HIDDEN REVIVALS AND THEIR SECRETS

MICHAEL MARCEL

Published by UK Wells.
Website: www.ukwells.org
Copyright © 2023 Michael Marcel
ISBN 978-1-910848-56-2

All rights reserved. No part of this publication can be reproduced, stored in a retrieval system, or transmitted in any form or by any means, electronic, mechanical, photocopying, recording or otherwise, without the prior written consent of the publisher. Short extracts may be quoted for review purposes.

Cover "Awakening' painting commissioned from Oliver Pengilley

Publishing services provided by
Publish My Book Limited
www.publishmybook.uk

Table of Contents

Introduction	5
1. Six Mile Water Revival	9
2. The Otley Revival	21
3. Tongues Revival	31
4. The 1858-64 Revival	51
5. 1873-75 Moody Awakening	89
6. The Rise of the Salvation Army	115
7. The Welsh Revival	165
8. The 1921 Forgotten Revival	187
9. The Hebrides Revival	197
Conclusion	209

The stories in this book are based on the scripts used to create a series of films currently available under the "Films" sections of www.ukwells.org

Introduction

Of the nine revivals/awakenings mentioned in this book, you will probably have only heard of two or three of them. Many have been hidden in history, either because the enemy did not want them found or nobody has looked through history to find them or once found they have not been published far and wide.

Secrets are hidden within these revivals and I try to reveal them in this book. There are also myths which have come about through inaccurate reporting, and I try to unravel these so you understand the truth.

Definition of Revival

Virtually every move of God you read about is called a 'revival'. There are exceptions, 'The Great Awakening' and the second, third, and fourth Great Awakenings, but the remainder are called 'revivals.' In most contexts 'revival' meant a 'revival of religion'.

It must be remembered that for a long time everybody went to church on Sunday or they were fined. So, when a revival came to a community it touched almost everyone as they had been brought up with religion as a greater or lesser part of their lives, so when a revival came, religion was revived in many.

However, everything changed in the 20th century as church attendance and Christian education declined rapidly. Now when a move of God arrives in a church it only touches a small percentage of the community. So, what are we now to call a move of God that comes to a church?

Introduction

There was a temptation to say that we must drop the word 'revival' completely, as it really only relates to the few people who just turn up at church. Since the word has been used universally for centuries, it would be difficult to drop it.

Therefore, my suggestion is to give a general move of God the name 'revival', but break it down as follows:

- Refreshing/Renewal. When there is an outpouring which touches active Christians in the church.
- Revival. When the move of God touches the 'backslidden'.
- Awakening. When the revival moves out beyond the church to the unsaved or when the unsaved come to the church and are 'awakened' to their sins and the existence and love of God. A problem with this is that the word 'awakening' has up until now been used to describe a worldwide revival, such as The Great Awakening of the 1730s, but this is a new day.
- Reformation. When the outpouring is so extensive that the society of the town/region/nation is reformed. Characteristics of this will be pubs and bars closing, crime markedly decreasing and laws changing.
- Transformation. When 80-100% of the people in an area are saved and Christianity pervades every area of society.

You will find that definitions of these words will vary greatly depending on who you speak to or the country you are from, so it is important that in conversation we clearly define our terms. My own preference is to talk about an 'Awakening', because that is what we need to change the nation.

An example of what I mean is The Toronto Blessing (1994). Using the criteria above, I would definitely call this move of God a 'Refreshing'. The Toronto Airport Christian Fellowship was inundated with British pastors and hungry Christians

Introduction

wanting to see God move. They brought the Toronto Blessing back to the United Kingdom, and it influenced many in the Body of Christ.

There are two types of revivals - one through evangelists who carry an anointing and one that comes through a revival atmosphere over a church or an area. An example of the former is George Jeffreys. Jeffreys was an evangelist who was saved in the Welsh Revival of 1904. He would go to a town, hire a room and start meetings. Because of what he carried, many were saved and often a church was formed before he left for pastures new. They became the Elim denomination.

The second type are described in this book. It tells the story of nine revivals/awakenings that we have had in the United Kingdom. From them I hope we can learn lessons on how to usher in a revival, how to maintain a revival and how to avoid the pitfalls that others have experienced.

We desperately need a new Great Awakening; one that will sweep the world like never before. In England we have not had an Awakening for over a hundred years and like thousands of others I have been praying for one for decades.

Many people seem to think that you pray for a revival and then wait for God to do something – no, that is not how it works. We need to recognise what God has planned and then step into His plan. We are in a season where an Awakening is on offer, so understanding what God wants of us is critical and then we need to do it!

I hope this book about the history of the United Kingdom will give you ideas of how to break through to fulfil your destiny.

Chapter One

Six Mile Water Revival
1625-35

The Six Mile Water stretches from Larne on the east coast of Ulster (the six counties of Northern Ireland plus three in Ireland) to Antrim on the shores of Lough Neagh. It is called 'Six Mile Water' due to a ford in the river being six miles from Carrickfergus and six miles from Antrim.

Two Ulster Earls, being on the losing side during a war, fled to mainland Europe with many other nobles in 1607; thus giving up their title to vast lands in Ulster. In 1609 the English government began a colonisation of Ulster, which was Catholic, rural and the spoke Gaelic. They saw it as an opportunity to anglicise, civilise and control an area that had proved difficult in the past. The British tenants were expected to be Protestant, English speaking and loyal to the King.

The state of religion in Ulster at the start of the seventeenth century was dreadful. Churches were in ruins; clergy were often non-resident and the province experienced frequent rebellions. The Reformation had failed because the Bible was not translated into Gaelic until 1602, and the clergy who were appointed were of poor quality. They were considered on a par with their flock, who largely came from Scotland and England and who were the dregs of society, murderers, thieves' adulterers etc. This may have been an exaggeration as clearly there were some roses amongst the thorns.

A few Presbyterians were appointed ministers in the district. In 1613 Edward Brice was appointed to Ballycarry; Robert Cunningham arrived at Holywood in 1615 and in 1619 John Ridge, an English Puritan, became vicar of Antrim. From 1621 some excellent ministers came from Scotland to avoid persecution there. From 1621 King James I imposed a set of rules on the Scottish Church that were intolerable to many of the clergy, these included confirmation by bishops.

Included amongst the Scottish clergy who arrived were:

- Robert Blair, vicar at Bangor; He was born in 1593 in Irvine. He was a licensed preacher and a professor at Glasgow University;
- George Dunbar was the vicar at Larne;
- Josiah Welch (Welsh) was the grandson of John Knox and the son of the revivalist John Welsh of Ayr. He was educated in Geneva until 1617 and was a professor at Glasgow University. He had to resign because of his Presbyterian beliefs. Robert Blair recommended he went to Ulster to minister at Templepatrick;
- John Livingstone born in 1603 in Kilsyth. He studied theology at St Andrew's University and was licensed in 1625. He went to Ulster in 1630 and ministered at Killinchy.

In Ulster, at this time, these ministers were beyond the reach of the persecution of James I, as the King was not interested in Ireland for now, but this situation would change later. They were all nominally Anglicans, but in their hearts they were Presbyterians; believers in rule by the Presbytery rather than by bishop.

James Glendinning was the minister of Carnmoney and a lecturer at Carrickfergus, the largest town in the Ulster. He got quite a reputation as a preacher, so Robert Blair went over to hear him. He wrote:

"About that time I heard of one James Glendinning, lecturer at Carrickfergus, who got no small applause there for being a learned man - I longed to hear him, and one morning I travelled from Bangor to Carrickfergus by water, and hearing him, I perceived he was careless in citing learned authors whom he had never seen nor read. After the sermon I waited for him and spoke with him, asking him if he thought he did honour to these people? He was quickly convinced and told me he had a vicarage in the country, to which he would go immediately."

Glendinning was a man of limited gifts, and Robert Blair thought that he was incapable of ministering to the sophisticated people of Carrickfergus. Taking Blair's advice Glendinning moved to a country parish, Oldstone, just south of Antrim, where he was amongst his own kind.

In Oldstone, Glendinning preached the law and the wrath of God if the law was broken, and a writer of the time commented that this was about all he was capable of preaching. Not on the face of it a very good mix for the Lord to pour out His blessings but pour them out He did in 1625. (I believe that when the atmosphere of revival is present subjects can be preached which would not be successful at other times.)

Multitudes became convicted of their sin through his teaching, with "a dozen in one day carried out as dead." The preaching of the law opened people's eyes to their sinfulness, and thinking they were damned many cried out "what must I do to be saved?" Many lay on the floor, convicted of their sin, but did not know how to find Jesus. However, Glendinning could not apply the Gospel to the sin-burdened hearts of the colonists. He could awaken them to their sin, but not show them the way to forgiveness through Jesus.

Fortunately, Josiah Welch had recently come to Ulster and he was skilled in doing what Glendinning could not and he went to help with the joyous work. Sadly, the success of the work went to Glendinning's head and he began to go into doctrinal error. His friends sent for Robert Blair to try to get him back on track. Blair wrote, "The journey being consider¬able I made such haste to obey their wishes that I stayed not so much as to have breakfast, and yet, before I could reach them, the night had fallen." Glendinning and his wife were in the care of a religious family, as their own house had been burned down some time previously. Blair refers to his vain efforts to convince Glendinning of his errors and foibles, concluding, "he, falling from error to error, did run away at last to see the seven Churches of Asia." This was around 1630.

The revival spread from County Antrim into County Down and even beyond the borders of these counties. John Livingstone gives an account of the effect of the revival:

> "Many of those who professed to be religious had been both ignorant and profane, and for being in debt and poverty, and worse causes, had left Scotland; yet the Lord was pleased by His word to work such a change. I do not think there were more lively and experienced Christians anywhere than were these at that time in Ireland, and that in good numbers, and many of them persons of a good outward condition in the world."

All classes of people were changed, and the reformation of society was noticeable for some time. Part of the change was a desire of the converts to learn more about God, so a 'Monthly Lecture Meeting' was started in Antrim.

The meeting was held on the last Friday of each month. Ministers came from County Antrim and County Down, including Welch, Blair, Hamilton, Cunningham, Dunbar and later, Livingstone. They met at Antrim Castle on the Thursday to discuss matters that concerned them; this was in effect a Presbytery meeting. Then on the Friday they taught at what was really a Bible school. There was prayer and fasting and four sermons at the summer meetings and three in the winter, and crowds came from all over to hear the Word of God. These meetings carried on until at least 1634 and helped spread the Gospel through the whole country. The meetings proved to be vital, in the long term, for the continuing faith of the people of Ulster. When persecution removed all their leaders from them, they were able to continue in small groups, teaching and encouraging one another.

Communion was usually served in a neighbouring parish on the Sunday following the Meetings. This was a three-day event with preparation on Saturday, Communion on Sunday and Thanksgiving on Monday. John Livingstone writes about the Communion:

> "I have known some who have come several miles from their own houses to communions, to the Saturday sermon, and spent the whole Saturday night in several groups, sometimes a minister being with them, sometimes themselves alone in discussion and prayer, and waited on the public ordinances the whole Sabbath, and spent the Sabbath night likewise, and yet at the Monday sermon despite sleeplessness... In these days it was no great difficulty for a minister to preach or pray in public or private, such was the hunger of the hearers."

People flocked to these services. Josiah Welch wrote as late as 1632 that he had around fifteen hundred at the services.

Six Mile Water Revival

In the midst of revival there was, as usual, persecution. Attacks came from conforming Anglican clergy, Catholic friars, Baptists and an Armenian. It was usually Blair who defended the revival, and he always won the argument. Disputes arose over the manifestations that occurred in some of the services, especially in Ballycarry. Many were 'slain in the Spirit' and one observer notes, "I have seen them myself stricken and swoon with the word - yes, a dozen in one day carried out of doors as dead...the power of God smiting their hearts for sin."

Most of the ministers were against the manifestations; wanting to conduct the services in an orderly manner. Now some of these manifestations will undoubtedly have come out of the flesh, but others would have been from the Holy Spirit, but they did not recognise the difference.

Blair attributed the manifestations to the work of Satan:

> "In the midst of the Public Worship these persons fell mourning and some of them were afflicted with pangs like convulsions, and daily the number of them increased. At first both the pastor and people, pitying them, had charitable thoughts, thinking it probable that it was the work of the Lord; but afterwards in a discussion they could find nothing to confirm these charitable thoughts = they could neither perceive any sense of their sinfulness, nor any panting after a Saviour. So the minister of the place did write some of his brethren to come over and examine the matter. Coming and conferring with these persons, we understood it to be a mere delusion and cheat of Satan to slander and disgrace the work of the Lord."

One of the Archbishop of Canterbury's followers, Henry Leslie, Dean of Down, wrote in 1631 about the revival, not surprisingly in an uncomplimentary way:

> "The people in that place are grown into such hysteria that the like is not to be found even among Anabaptists, for there is spoken a new theology that no man can be counted converted unless he feels the pains of his new birth such as St Paul felt. So that every sermon, 40 or so people, for the most part women, fall down in the church in a trance. and are (as it is supposed) senseless, but in their fits they are badly afflicted with convulsions, shakings, unnatural motions. After they awake, they confess that they have seen demons and from then on they put on such a mark of austerity that they are never seen to laugh, and never talk of anything but God, though so idly that they always take his name in vain."

One needs to take this statement with a pinch of salt as Leslie is trying to turn things to his own advantage.

Four hundred years ago there were manifestations of Holy Spirit, and all through that time to this day some people have believed that manifestations are not of the Lord!

Robert Echlin, bishop of Down, was at first supportive of the Presbyterian ministers, but changed his attitude towards them. The Irish archbishop, James Ussher remained supportive, refusing to bow under the pressure which was mounting against them.

In 1630 Blair went to Scotland where he visited John Livingstone. They ended up at Kirk of Shotts where they conducted a service which became known as the Kirk of Shotts Revival. Two Scottish ministers accused them of 'exciting people to ecstasies and teaching the necessity of bodily pains to attest the reality of the new birth' and reported them to Henry Leslie, who passed the accusations on to Bishop Echlin. In late summer 1631 Blair, Livingstone, Dunbar and Welch were suspended. Their friends appealed to Ussher who ordered Echlin to withdraw the suspension. The case was appealed to London to the intolerant Archbishop Laud. Through Laud's influence Blair, Welch, Livingstone, and Dunbar were brought to trial, but they refused to conform to Episcopacy (the government of a Church by bishops) so they were deposed from ministry in 1632. Blair went to London to appeal to King Charles I (he had succeeded his father James I) and he ordered the Lord Deputy of Ireland, Wentworth, to retry the case.

The four ministers continued to preach until Blair met with Wentworth in the latter half of 1634. Wentworth spoke against the Church of Scotland and upbraided Blair. The situation became so dark for the Presbyterians of Ulster that they began to look towards America to escape persecution. Livingstone and another were commissioned to go to America to find a place for settlement, but whilst in Plymouth some things deterred them from completing their mission and they returned home. For political reasons, in May 1634, Wentworth instructed Echlin to withdraw the suspension of the four men for six months.

During this time the ministers carried on their work in any place they could. Josiah Welch stood at the back door of his house to preach to the people in his house and in the garden. The Bishop of Derry appealed to Wentworth as to the danger of allowing Presbyterians to preach and they were suspended again in November. Soon after this Welch and Echlin died and Dunbar returned to Scotland.

Blair and Livingstone, with one hundred and forty others, built a ship to take them beyond persecution to America. They planned to sail in the spring when the weather was good, but delays meant that the 'Eagle Wing' did not sail until the autumn. Fierce storms damaged their ship and taking all the difficulties they had experienced as a sign that God did not want them to go, they returned to Ulster in November 1636. They carried on ministering to the people, but on hearing they were going to be arrested, Blair and Livingstone returned to their native Scotland in 1637.

On the 11th-12th August 1636, the Bishop of Down tried Hamilton, Cunningham, Ridge and Calvert at the old Belfast Parish Church in front of bishops, nobles, gentry and clergy. Brice died before he could be tried. They were all banned from preaching in the diocese, for the sin of not accepting Episcopacy. In response to their sentence Cunningham said:

> "I have now lived these twenty years amongst you in this kingdom, serving the Lord in His holy ministry, and believed I would spend the rest of my days here, which cannot be very long, for my body is very weak. My doctrine and life for that time are known to most who are here present. I appeal to all their consciences if they can say anything against me in either of them. I always kept myself close to the commission of my Lord. But now I am required to receive restrictions on my ministry which are against my conscience. I would rather lay down my ministry at the feet of my Lord and Saviour Christ, from whom I received it, than to live with an evil conscience in the free liberty of it."

What an amazing remark! They all returned to Scotland with some of their followers in 1638.

Those colonists who remained in Ulster were forced to accept the Episcopal forms of worship or carry out their own services in secret, much as the Covenantors did later in Scotland. It seems that many continued on the path laid out by the Scottish ministers as Livingstone records that five hundred of his old flock came over to his new parish

Six Mile Water Revival

of Stranraer to celebrate Communion. Many of Blair's flock visited him for services when he was living in Irvine. The revival went on for at least ten years and may have gone on beyond 1636. This is a long time for a revival, so the effect of the Six Mile Water Revival must have been great. Through it, Presbyterianism was firmly rooted in Ulster and despite many ups and downs it lasts to this day.

There is a very sad postscript to this story. A Catholic uprising in 1641, caused by their anger at their land being taken by the colonists, saw approximately four thousand colonists killed in Ulster.

As mentioned, Robert Blair and John Livingstone returned to Scotland in 1637, going to their friend David Dickson, vicar at Irvine, who employed and protected them from the authorities. Blair went on to be an important figure in Scotland, becoming Moderator of the Church of Scotland until he was imprisoned by Charles II. He died in 1666.

John Livingstone also became a significant figure in Scotland. As a condition of Charles II being offered the crown, Livingstone accepted his oath to give freedom of worship to the people. Within a few years of becoming king, Charles broke his word and persecuted many Christians. Charles banished him to Rotterdam for the last ten years of his life.

Robert Cunningham, who said in his farewell speech that he did not expect to live very long, also came to Irvine, but died soon after arriving. After his death he was called by the ecclesiastical authorities in Ulster to come before them. For not appearing he was heavily fined and his widow and eight children had their possessions seized to pay the fine.

David Dickson, was at Irvine for twenty-three years. He became Moderator of the Church Assembly twice and was

Chair of Divinity at Edinburgh University before. In 1662, like his good friends Blair and Livingstone, he was thrown out of the church by Charles II, a few months before he died.

These men lived through tumultuous times, perhaps the most tumultuous in Scottish church history, but they overcame their persecution and shone brightly, they are still remembered 400 years later.

Conclusion

It is worth remembering these ministers went to Ulster to escape persecution. To begin with they were able to run their churches as they pleased, but when pressure came from the bishops for them to conform, they never compromised, preferring trial and banishment from their parishes for truth's sake. They were brave men! There is too little truth and too much compromise these days.

Puritans in seventeenth century Britain, who today would probably be called charismatics or evangelicals, were persecuted for most of the century under James I, Charles I and Charles II. Some left in the Mayflower to go to America, and they were followed by many more.

With what is happening in the societies where most of us live in the West, I have no doubt that we will be experiencing significant religious persecution in the near future. Will we compromise or will we be like these brave men who fixed their eyes on Jesus and refused to bow under the persecuting government of those days?

Much of the above was taken from 'The Six Mile Water Revival of 1625' by W D Baillie, published by The Presbyterian Historical Society of Ireland.

Chapter Two

The Otley Revival
1758-62

I came across an article in a Methodist magazine a long time ago. I was shocked by its contents. It describes a revival in Otley that virtually nobody knew about, yet John Wesley thought it was the most important of his life. It was the first time, as far as I am aware, that the Baptism of Fire/Sanctification/Holiness became generally accepted anywhere in the world. It is amazing that such a significant event should become almost entirely unknown in the United Kingdom.

The article said: "Many years since, I saw that 'without holiness no man shall see the Lord.' I began following after it – and ten years later, God gave me a clearer view than I had before of the way how to attain this, namely, by faith in the Son of God."

These were the opening words of a letter written in 1771 by John Wesley to Lady Huntingdon. The letter is an important one, relative both to his own experience and to his preaching of entire sanctification. In the remainder of the letter, he reminds her ladyship that for more than thirty years, he has continued to preach: "We are saved from sin, we are made holy by fire."

Background

The "many years since" take us back to 1725-29. This saw the rise of Oxford Methodism, a band of young men earnestly seeking God and holiness. John Wesley was their leader and it was typical of Wesley, the scholar, that books influenced him greatly in his quest for holiness. The writings of Clemens' Alexandrinus, Bishop Taylor, Thomas a Kempis, William Law, Fenelo and the mystics convinced him that holiness was of the hear'; it was rooted in heavenly character and sanctified thoughts and did not merely consist, as he had earnestly believed, in outwar' works of righteousness.

In 1738, Wesley saw what his greatest mentor, William Law had not seen, that salvation was by faith alone. Justification and sanctification are received by faith. "We are saved from sin; we are made holy, by faith." Wesley immediately declared the gospel of faith and soon all over the land hundreds of people could testify to its reality. There were fewer testimonies to sanctification than to justification, but many were seeking the blessing, and some had entered into the experience. Wesley at first seems to have thought that the blessing was attainable only at death, but he soon realised that what God could do at the hour of death, He could do, a week, a year, ten years, before.

In Wesley's Journals there are records of those who were entirely sanctified. On Saturday, April 16, 1757, Wesley talked with M. B., "a mother in Israel," who told Wesley:

> "On August 23, 1744, I was sitting alone, about eight in the morning - when the power of God came upon me so that I shook all over like a leaf. Then a voice said: 'This day is salvation come to thy house.' At that instant, I felt an entire change. I was full of love and full of God. I had the witness in myself that He had made an end of sin and taken my whole heart forever. And from that moment I have never lost the witness, nor felt anything, in my heart but pure love."

The Otley Revival

Here is as plain a testimony to entire sanctification as can be found anywhere in Wesley's writings. On November 1, 1762, Wesley wrote: "I have known and taught instantaneous sanctification above these twenty years." Wesley would not have continued to preach entire sanctification by faith for "above twenty years" if there had been no witnesses to it all this time.

Wesley's sermon "On Patience," published in 1784, is a much neglected source of his teaching on sanctification. He says:

> "Two or three persons in London (in 1744) gave me an account of their experiences. It was exactly similar to the preceding account of entire sanctification," (i.e., instantaneous).

Records show that in 1756 John Wesley and others again took great care to examine each witness individually and we were fully persuaded they did not deceive themselves.

The Revival

1760 saw the starting point of the "glorious work of sanctification," This revival, which began in 1758, is what John Wesley called the "Methodist Pentecost." Here is his account of it:

> "In the beginning of the year 1760, there was a great revival of the work of God in Yorkshire. On January 13th, says a correspondent, "about-thirty persons were met together, in Otley (near Leeds, in Yorkshire) in the evening, in order, as usual, to pray, sing hymns, and to provoke one another to love and good works. When they came to speak of the several states of their souls, some with deep sighs and groans complained of the heavy burden they felt from the remains of inbred sin; seeing in

a clearer light than ever before the necessity of a deliverance from it... They had no doubt of the favour of God, but they could not rest while they had anything in them contrary to His nature. One cried out in an agony, 'Lord, deliver me from my sinful nature,' then a second, a third, and a fourth; and while he that prayed first was uttering these words, 'Thou God of Abraham, Isaac and Jacob, hear us for the sake of thy Son Jesus,' one broke out: 'Blessed be the Lord forever; for He has purified my heart,' Another, 'Praise the Lord with me, for He has cleansed my heart from sin.' Thus they continued for the space of two hours, some praising and magnifying God, some crying to Him for pardon or purity of heart, with the greatest agony of spirit. Before they parted, three believed God had fulfilled His word and cleansed them from all unrighteousness."

Wesley visited Otley and was convinced of the genuineness of the reports. He speaks of the revival at Otley "as the work that had been nearly at a stand."

This revival in 1760 was the most important of its kind Wesley experienced in fifty-three years of evangelism. There had been other revivals, like those in the 1730s, 1740s and Weardale in 1772, but none so deep, so far-reaching, and so lasting as that at Otley.

Its effects were soon felt all over England and in the south and west of Ireland. On October 28, 1762, John Wesley wrote:

"Many years ago my brother frequently said, 'Your day of Pentecost is not fully come, but I doubt not it will. And you will then hear of persons sanctified, as frequently as you do now of persons justified.' Any unprejudiced reader may observe that it was now fully come. And accordingly, we did hear of persons sanctified, in London and most other parts of England, and in Dublin and many other places in Ireland, as frequently as of persons justified; although instances of the latter were far more frequent than they had been for twenty years before."

The Methodist Pentecost had come! If John Wesley, always exact and definitive in his use of words, likened the work at Otley to that which launched the church in Jerusalem, then we can be sure it was a revival of importance. Wherever the flame spread, hundreds were converted and many experienced the blessing of entire sanctification.

The following quotations from Wesley's writings are representative of many more that clearly indicate, in Wesley's own expression, "the word of God as fire among the stubble."

March 6, 1761: "I met again with those who believe God has delivered them from the root of bitterness. Their number increases daily. I know not if fifteen or sixteen have not received the blessing this week."

September 21, 1761: "Here likewise [at Bristol] I had the satisfaction to observe a considerable increase of the work of God. The congregations were very large and the people hungering and thirsting after righteousness, and every day afforded us fresh instances of people convicted of sin or converted to God. So that it seems God was pleased to pour out His Spirit this year, on every part both of England and Ireland; perhaps in a manner we had never seen before, certainly not for twenty years."

July 24, 1762: "I rode to Dublin and found the flame was not only continuing but increasing." The revival at Dublin was so extensive that Wesley gave an account of it in detail. He concluded: "In some respect, the work of God in this place was more remarkable than even that in London. It is far greater, in proportion to the time, and to the number of people", A few days later Wesley, heard of a similar work in Limerick, in the west of Ireland. "There is a glorious work going on in Limerick. The Lord has made your last visit to us a great blessing. Such times were never before in Limerick. The fire which broke out before you left us is now spreading on every side".

John Wesley returned to England to find the 'River of Blessing' in full spate. From Cheshire, he heard that "there was an outpouring of the Spirit - nor is His hand yet stayed". "The power of God is present with us - six or seven justified in a week; others find the very remains of sin destroyed" - this was the encouraging news from Staffordshire.

On August 4, 1762, Wesley rode to Liverpool, where "there was such a work of God as had never been known there before." Two days later he heard from Bolton: "Glory be to God, He is doing wonders among us." The next day Wesley found sixty at Manchester who "believed God had cleansed their hearts."

At the close of 1762, Wesley reflected:

> "I now stood and looked back on the past year; a year of uncommon trials and uncommon blessings. Abundance have been convinced of sin, very many have found peace with God; and in London only, I believe full two hundred have been brought into glorious liberty"

After 1760 all the Methodist societies in England and Ireland felt the influence of the Otley revival for many years. In that year the total number joined in all the societies could not have been more than 13,000. In 1767 the number had risen to 26,341, and in 1771 to 30,338. On November 18, 1763, Wesley wrote:

> ".... God began that great work which has continued ever since, without any considerable intermission... The peculiar work of this season has been what St Paul calls 'the perfecting of the saints.' Many persons in various parts of England and Ireland have experienced so deep and universal a change, as it had not before entered into their hearts to conceive.... The work of God went on. Nor has it ceased to this day in any of its branches: God still convinces, justifies, sanctifies."

Eighteen years later, Wesley's judgment had not changed. In 1781 he wrote:

> "The glorious work of sanctification spread from 1760, first through various parts of Yorkshire, afterward in London... Dublin... and all the south and west of Ireland. And wherever the work of sanctification increased, the whole work of God increased in all its branches"

The revival in Otley was convincing proof that when believers entered the blessing of entire sanctification the whole work of God prospered. John Wesley saw this in most of his societies; when believers claimed the blessing, sinners were converted. His Journals have much to say on the relationship between entire sanctification and revival.

September 15, 1762: "Where Christian perfection is not strongly and clearly enforced, the believers grow dead and cold."

September 30, 1765: "Where Christian perfection is little insisted upon, be the preachers ever so eloquent, there is little increase, either in the number or grace of the hearers.

The Otley Revival

February 8, 1766: "Where Christian perfection is not strongly and explicitly preached, there is seldom any remarkable blessing from God, and consequently, little addition to the society, and little life in the members of it... Till you press the believers to expect full salvation now, you must not look for any revival."

After analysing the influence and extent of the Otley revival, it is significant that it had little or no effect on Scotland. The chief reason was that Calvinism in Scotland did not respond too readily to the Arminian preachers and especially their teaching on Christian perfection. Wesley only makes four references to sanctification in Scotland.

June 8, 1779: "I spent some time with the society [at Inverness], increased from twelve to between fifty and sixty... Many were going on to perfection, so that all the pains which have been taken to stop the work of God here, have hitherto been in vain."

June 17, 1779: "When Mr. Brackenbury preached the old Methodist doctrine [in Edinburgh] one of them said: 'You must not preach such doctrine here. The doctrine of perfection is not calculated for the meridian of Edinburgh.' Is it any wonder that the work of God has not prospered here?"

Sanctification and revival are inextricably linked together.

Conclusion

We, today, who are committed to this gospel of entire sanctification can learn much from the Methodist Pentecost. We must learn, with John Wesley, "that until we press the believers to expect full salvation now, we must not look for any revival."

Many of Wesley's leaders rejected the idea of sanctification and stopped teaching it, so the movement stopped for many years in England. However, Wesley sent Francis Asbury and Thomas Coke to America to lead the 'Methodists' there. Both were strong believers in sanctification and taught about it in America. From my studies I have not found a mention of sanctification in the United Kingdom until the visit of the American revivalist James Caughey in 1841. It was Caughey who strongly influenced William Booth, who made holiness an important aspect of the Salvation Army.

I cannot overstate the importance of this revival. Holiness is absolutely the key to revival; if we have clean hands and a pure heart the Lord can use us to bring revival to the nation. The fact that this biblical truth was lost until 1758 and then intermittently lost until today, is no coincidence. The enemy knows how important holiness is and will do anything to stop it. For the last hundred years there has been little taught about Sanctification; this needs to change!

I have written a booklet on the Baptism of Fire (Holiness) which is available as a free download from my website ukwells.org.

I am grateful for permission to quote from "Studies in the Methodist Revival" by Herbert McGonigle, in "The Nazarene Preacher Magazine, March 1967."

There are many quotes from Wesley's Journal.

Chapter Three

Tongues Revival
1827-30

The story is quite complicated, so it is helpful if I begin by listing the main participants:

- John MacLeod Campbell - Church of Scotland minister of Row (Rhu) Church.
- Alexander J Scott - Campbell's assistant and then works with Edward Irving in London.
- Mary and Isabella Campbell - sisters living in Rosneath
- Robert Story - Church of Scotland minister of Rosneath parish, next door to Rhu,
- James and George Macdonald - Brothers living in Port Glasgow.
- Margaret Macdonald - Sister of James and George in Port Glasgow.
- Edward Irving - Church of Scotland minister in London.
- Henry Drummond - Banker in Albury, Surrey who co-founded the Catholic Apostolic Church.

The uniqueness of this revival is that it included the revelation of two new theologies. The first was that salvation was available to all as opposed to the general view of the Church of Scotland that it was only available to the 'elect'. The second was that the Gifts of the Spirit were available 'today'.

It was also, I believe, the first occasion where the gift of tongues, the interpretation of tongues and the speaking of prophecy were seen in the United Kingdom. There may have been the odd individual moving in the gift in the past, but not a general experience as happened here.

Another very interesting feature of this revival is how the enemy succeeded in snuffing it out completely and it would be another seventy-five years before the United Kingdom experienced the gift of tongues widely again (after the Azusa Street revival of 1906).

The story begins with the appointment of John MacLeod Campbell as minister of Rhu in 1825. He was very concerned about the state of religion in his parish which was at a very low ebb. At the time, there were generally two types of ministers in Scotland; the Moderates, who believed that the morality of a person was his main concern, so he seldom preached on salvation; and the Evangelicals, who normally preached a sermon that dealt too much in grim and narrow self-inspection. The situation was improving as the Haldane brothers had been changing Scottish churches since 1799, with James spreading revival and Robert building churches and training future ministers.

Robert Story, minister of Rosneath parish wrote:

> "Campbell's predecessor was a man of superior gifts, a good scholar, and of more than the average accomplishment of the ministers of his day. He was, however, a cold intellectual preacher, rather inclined to repress anything in the form of enthusiasm of feeling, than attempt to stir up any great earnestness in the religious tone of the people. With few exceptions, indeed, it may be stated, that religion was at a low ebb throughout the families of the parish. Mr Campbell having entered upon his parochial charge with a deep sense of the responsibility of his office, and with a single-minded desire to devote all his energies to the

accomplishment of its duties, felt, upon surveying the condition of the parish, that every effort must be made to awaken an interest in the great things that belonged to his people's peace, and to rouse them from a state of what seemed such spiritual carelessness and insensibility.

Campbell shut himself up in his study with only his Bible and Concordance, and with weapons drawn from that armoury only, in the strength and by the counsel of his Master, determined to make war upon the enemy of truth, and rouse the immortal souls committed to his pastoral charge from their deep and perilous slumber. Week after week, so prepared for his public ministrations, it may be easily imagined what freshness and vitality there must have been in his presentation of the truth to his audience, urged, as it was, with intense earnestness of manner."

His studies led Campbell to the belief that salvation was available to all. This was radical in Scotland at the time as the Calvinist view was only the elect could be saved. With this revelation in mind, he began to preach on subjects that might awaken his congregation to the idea of sin in their lives and lead them to the idea that they must be born again. He told them that anyone who turned from sin would at once be embraced by a loving God. He also preached on the love of the Father which was very different from the dour preaching of the day.

Around 1827, this different kind of preaching stirred up the neighbourhood and a revival began. 'There was an awakening of religious life there which got its first impulse from the Rhu Kirk. Greenock, Glasgow, Edinburgh thrilled as with the gush of a fresh spring-tide.' (Albury Apostles, 'The story of the body known as the Catholic Apostolic Church', by Rowland A Davenport).

At this time Alexander Scott preached his first sermon after his ordination and John Campbell was impressed by his assistant, so Scott remained for a short time to assist Campbell in his ministry. Scott too had begun to believe that salvation was available to all, but there began to form in his mind a new revelation, that the Gifts of the Spirit were available for now and were not just for apostolic times.

Meanwhile, a banker, Henry Drummond, had bought an estate in Albury, near Guildford and from 1826-30, he had an annual conference made up of evangelical leaders. It was known as the Albury Circle. The main theological input came from Edward Irving, who was the minister at the National Scotch Church in Regent's Square, London. These meetings concentrated on praying for a great outpouring of Holy Spirit.

During 1827/8, Robert Story was ill and travelled to visit Drummond and Irving. He was stirred by the conference he attended at Albury and spent time, much as John Campbell did, re-evaluating his understanding of the Gospels. They came to the same conclusion, that salvation was open to all.

While Story was away, Campbell looked after his parish and his preaching made quite a stir in the district:

> "What we popularly term a revival, began in Rosneath; a revival, for which Mr Campbell's labours of love in Mr Story's absence had prepared the way, and which was now all the more thorough and lasting, that it entirely lacked the accompaniment of those painful and disorderly demonstrations, which have of late marked the progress of the so-called religious movements. There were no prostrations of the body, no outcries, no crowded midnight meetings, no public confessions and

details of conviction and conversion; there was a quiet, earnest, prayerful seeking after God's truth - a vivid enlightenment - a living reformation. Nor was this confined to the members of his own flock merely - others elsewhere hearing of the work that was going on, came to witness it and to share the blessing."

Many writers of the time were keen to show a revival was conducted in an 'orderly' way, without manifestations, inferring that such a revival was more genuine.

In March 1828 Robert Story wrote a pastoral letter to his people setting out his new theology, specifically, 'Believe that in Christ your sins are forgiven.' It too created quite a stir in the area.

In May/June that year, Edward Irving toured Dumfriesshire and the area around Rosneath and Rhu. Irving was a good looking man, very charismatic and a powerful preacher. Thousands came to hear him speak. One might think that the large numbers he attracted was due to his charisma, but I believe that it was more due to the revival atmosphere that pervaded the area. He met Alexander Scott and was so impressed that he asked him to come down to London to help him in his work; Scott agreed. Also, at this time it appears that Edward Irving had come to the same conclusion as Campbell, Scott and Story; that salvation was available to all by faith.

But the enemy began to move against these new revelations and the revival that was spreading. Local ministers were unhappy that teaching went away from the norm of salvation only for the elect:

> "Amid all opposition, Campbell's words had free course. The pulpits of the neighbouring clergy, one after another, were closed against Mr Campbell. The

Greenock ministers (not including Scott) refused to take part in the services of the Seaman's Chapel, in that port, if Messrs Campbell and Story were allowed at any time to officiate, and their names accordingly were struck off the list of officiating ministers. In every way, distrust and resistance were displayed, but still his teaching prevailed."

The next stage of this story begins with the life and death of Isabella Campbell, who lived at Fernicarry House at the edge of Robert Story's parish:

"[Isabella] was one of his Sunday school scholars, and was by him admitted to the Holy Communion, and after many a long and painful struggle, she was able in God's light to see light and to enter into the glorious liberty of His children. While yet a girl in her teens a pulmonary disease attacked her, and gradually reduced her so low that at last she was chained almost entirely to her home at Fernicarry. While there her minister saw her constantly, and while he helped to instruct and comfort her, his own spirit was much quickened by its interaction with hers; for during this illness she seemed step by step to enter into the very Holy of Holies, and to enjoy a most rapt and intense communion with her God and Saviour, to the peace and joy of which she bore perpetual witness by the exalted utterances of her faith and love. Her life was indeed hidden with Christ in God; its fountain was within the Veil; there, she felt as few are able to realise, were the realities, here the illusion. 'I am not conscious', says one who went, as many did for the truth's sake, to visit her on her dying bed, 'that I ever was made so to feel the reality of eternal things. When I rode away from the house, I actually felt as if the firmament overhead, and your mountains and the lake at our feet, and the very ground over which we were yet sensibly passing, were all elusive, and as if I could have put up my hand to push them all aside, to make room again for the great realities which I seemed to have left with that wonderful girl.'"

Isabella's life and death were an inspiration to many and people poured in to visit this godly girl. She died in November 1828 and Story wrote a short memoir about her – "The Memoir of Isabella":

"...though almost studiously divested of literary grace, or any interest external to herself, depicted a life so consecrated by suffering, by faith, by prayer, by rapt, almost mystic, communion with its Divine source, that it produced a very vivid impression. It was widely read in England and Scotland and was promptly reprinted in America, where it also had a wide circulation. To how many it was made by God's Spirit a messenger of peace and salvation, His day shall reveal; but even had it produced no effect, except in those cases which became personally known to its author, the result would have been richly ample."

This memoir added to the revival that was going on, further stirring the population.

At the end of 1829, Scott came up to Scotland and spoke for John Campbell at Rhu and Port Glasgow, speaking for the first time on the Gifts of the Spirit being available for today:

"Religion had at this crisis taken a hold on the entire mind of the population, which it very seldom possesses. It was not only the inspiration of their hearts but the subject of their thoughts, discussions, and conversations. They seem not only to have been stimulated in personal piety but occupied to an almost unprecedented degree with those spiritual concerns which are so generally kept altogether separate from the common tide of life. On such a state of mind Mr Scott's pregnant suggestion fell with the force that might have been expected from it. That which to the higher intelligence was a matter of theoretical belief became in other hands an active principle, wildly productive, and with many unpremeditated and unforeseen results." ('The Life of Edward Irving.' Volume 2, page 107, by Mrs Oliphant).

Early in 1830, Isabella's sister, Mary, developed the same terminal disease as her sister (large abscesses on the lungs). Like her sister she spent a lot of time seeking God. She became locally famous from selling the memoir about her sister and had many visitors at Fernicarry.

Mary had heard Edward Irving speaking about healing and she had heard Scott teaching on the Gifts of the Spirit late in 1829 when he was visiting his father's manse in Greenock. One Sunday Mary was suddenly filled with Holy Spirit and spoke in tongues for about an hour:

> "It was on the Lord's Day; and one of her sisters, along with a female friend... had been spending the whole day in humiliation, and fasting, and prayer before God, with a special respect to the restoration of the gifts. They had come up in the evening to the sick bed of their sister... While they were praying, the Holy Ghost came with mighty power upon the sick woman as she lay in her weakness and she spoke at great length, and with superhuman strength, in an unknown tongue, to the astonishment of all who heard, and to her own great edification and enjoyment in God. She has told me that this first manifestation of the Spirit was

the strongest she ever had; and that it was in some degree necessary it should have been so, otherwise she would not have dared to give way to it." (*'The Life of Edward Irving.'* Volume 2, page 129, by Mrs Oliphant).

This was the beginning of the first move of God that released the gift of tongues in the United Kingdom.

The story now shifts to Port Glasgow where there were five Macdonald siblings living together. The two Macdonald brothers came to Jesus in 1828 and they started prayer meetings for the state of the Church and the world that were held two or three times a week. Their local minister spoke against them but they continued praying for revival. Having heard Alexander Scott preach they were praying for and expecting the restoration of Spiritual Gifts.

One of the three sisters, Margaret:

> "...for several days had been so unusually ill, that I (and the doctor) quite thought her dying.... Mrs -- and myself had been sitting quietly at her bedside when the power of the Spirit came upon her. She said, 'There will be a mighty baptism of the Spirit this day' and then broke out in a most marvellous setting forth of the wonderful works of God; and, as if her own weakness had been altogether lost in the strength of the Holy Ghost, continued, with little or no intermission, for two or three hours in a mixture of praise, prayer, and exhortation.' At dinner-time James and George (brothers) came home as usual, whom she then addressed at great length, concluding with a solemn prayer for James, that he might at that time be endowed with the power of the Holy Ghost. Almost instantly James calmly said, 'I have got it.' He walked to the window and stood silent for a minute or two. I looked at him, and

almost trembled, there was such a change upon his whole appearance. He then, with a step and manner of the most indescribable majesty, walked up to Margaret's bedside, and addressed her in those words of the twentieth Psalm, 'Arise, and stand upright.' He repeated the words, took her by the hand, and she got up... we all quietly sat down and had our dinner. After it, my brothers went to the building-yard, as usual, where James wrote to Miss Campbell, commanding her in the name of the Lord to arise. The next morning, after breakfast, James said, 'I am going down to the quay, to see if Miss Campbell is come across the water' at which we expressed our surprise, as he had said nothing to us of having written to her"

"On Wednesday I (Mary Campbell) did not feel quite so lethargic but was suffering some pain from breathing and palpitation of my heart. Two individuals who saw me about four hours before my recovery said that I would never be strong; that I was not to expect a miracle. Soon after that I received dear brother James McDonald's letter, giving an account of his sister being raised up, and commanding me to rise and walk... As I read, every word came home with power, and when I came to the command to rise, it came home with a power which no words can describe; I felt it to be the voice of Christ; it was such a voice as could not be resisted. A mighty power was instantaneously exerted upon me: I felt as if I had been lifted from off the earth, and all my diseases were taken from off me at the voice of Christ. I was actually made in a moment to stand on my feet, leap and walk, sing and rejoice." *(these last two paragraphs came from 'Memoirs of James and George Macdonald of Port Glasgow' by Robert Norton)*

Mary then crossed the loch and met an expectant James who was waiting at the dock:

> "After her restoration to health, Mary Campbell went to Helensburgh, where, in the summer of 1830, meetings were constantly held, amid much wonder and excitement, in which persons who were believed, and probably believed themselves to be, under the influence of the Spirit, spoke in tongues, interpreted, prophesied, etc. To these meetings, people came from Edinburgh and London, who, returning to their respective congregations inaugurated similar scenes in both these cities."

At the same time James and George Macdonald held daily meetings in Port Glasgow. One of the Macdonald sisters wrote a letter on 18th May 1830:

> "What wonderful things have taken place among us since I last wrote... I have thought of writing to you every day for some time, but since Miss Campbell was raised and the gift of tongues given, the house has been filled every day from all parts of England, Scotland and Ireland; some of them are people enquiring what must they do to be saved, but the greater part are Christians come to glorify God by witnessing what great things God is doing amongst us, and there are a few who have come to dispute and deny the gifts... One night at a prayer-meeting two persons were brought to know the Lord and are going on making progress in the life of God. Last Wednesday the gift of tongues was given to Miss -- and on Friday to our servant." *('Memoirs of James and George Macdonald of Port Glasgow' by Robert Norton)*

Tongues Revival

Meanwhile, the annual conferences were continuing at Albury in England and the news of the revival going on in Scotland came to the group. It seemed to be an answer to their prayers as they heard that speaking in tongues, healing and prophecy were being experienced there. At the final conference in July 1830, they decided to send six people to check it out to see if it was indeed a work of God.

One of their number, John Cardale, wrote in November 1830 in a Journal owned by the Albury Circle, a first-hand account of the meetings while visiting the Macdonalds:

> "Dear sir, You have requested me to state some particulars of what my five fellow-travellers and myself experienced during our recent stay at Port-Glasgow. I do not hesitate to comply; earnestly praying that the mere relating of facts may be made instrumental to the reception and understanding of the scriptural doctrine of the Holy Spirit, both in His power and in His love (for the Spirit is One), without which the manifestations, which we witnessed, of His gifts, will be but as an idle tale.
>
> We spent three weeks, arriving at the end of August in Port Glasgow and the neighbourhood, and attended the meetings regularly while there; the meetings were held every evening, and occasionally in the morning. The details of one of these meetings is the same as them all: I may just as well relate what took place at the first which we attended. Someone reads a Psalm, which is sung by the people there; then a chapter from the Bible and he then prays.
>
> On this occasion, after two other gentlemen, James Macdonald read and prayed. His prayer was most remarkable. The empathy with the mind of our

Saviour; interceding for a world which tramples on His blood and rejects His mercy, and for the church which grieves the Holy Ghost; the humiliation for sin, and the hungering after holiness, were totally different from anything I had ever before heard. He then, in the course of prayer, and while engaged in intercession for others, began speaking in an unknown tongue; and after speaking for some time he sang, or rather chanted, in the same tongue. He then rose, and we all rose with him; and, in a very loud voice and with great seriousness, he addressed us in the same tongue for a considerable time: he then, with the same loudness of voice and manner, addressed us in English, calling on us to prepare for trial, for we had great trials to go through for the testimony of Jesus; to crucify the flesh; to lay aside every weight; to put far from us our fleshly wisdom, power, and strength; and to keep us in our God.

After he had concluded, a short pause ensued when suddenly the woman-servant of the Macdonald's arose and spoke (for a space of, probably, ten minutes) in an unknown tongue, and then in English: the latter was entirely from Scripture, consisting of passages from different parts, and connected together in the most remarkable manner.

The meeting concluded with a psalm, a chapter, and prayer from another gentleman. Immediately on conclusion, Mrs --, one of the ladies who had received the Spirit, but had not received the gift of tongues (she received the gift while we were in the country) arose, went out of the room and began speaking in a loud voice of the coming judgments. After she had spoken about five minutes, Mr Macdonald started to speak, and Mrs -- instantly ceased speaking. It is impossible to describe the gravity and grandeur, both of words and manner, in which she gave testimony to the judgments coming on the earth; but also directed the church to the coming of the Lord as her hope of deliverance. When she had concluded, we left the house." *(These last paragraphs are from, The Morning Watch Journal, volume 2, pages 869-71)*

I am not sure how long the revival lasted in Scotland; somewhere it mentioned three years, but I have not seen any confirmation. It goes to Edward Irving's church in London (more later), but it is at this time (the end of 1830) that the opposition of the enemy really manifests. Obviously, something so new would bring opposition and so it did.

The attack was in two directions - against the ministers who preached that salvation was available for all and against the idea that people could speak in tongues or be healed. The most obvious person to attack was Mary Campbell. As the first person to receive tongues and the second to be healed in this move of God; if you could discredit her, you could argue against the whole movement. Unfortunately, Mary had weaknesses that made her an easy mark. Most of the criticism against her came from her own pastor, Robert Story.

In the biography by his son, Story suggests that Mary's head was turned by all the attention she received after the death of her sister. She later married and went down south to be with Irving. Story writes that Mary admitted to him that some of the prophecies she uttered were from her own imagination. I want to be generous towards her here because people in those days must have wondered what was going on if a prophecy they spoke was not fulfilled. They did not have the experience we have these days, knowing that we prophesy in part and that the timing of God is different from ours.

Once her own minister was known to question what happened to Mary, it was easy for others to do the same. Her healing and Margaret's were easily discarded by some by saying that they were on the mend anyway. I think it unfair to discard what happened to Mary. She may have not had a perfect character but I do not think that diminishes what she experienced which was witnessed by several people.

What happened to the Macdonald siblings was less easy to dismiss by the detractors. From what I have read they were held in high esteem throughout the area.

The Church of Scotland did the enemy's work quite well, moving against the ministers involved. In 1831 the General Assembly found John Campbell guilty of teaching heretical doctrines and deprived him of his living. His heresy was saying that salvation was available to all. Robert Story very nearly received the same fate as his friend. He defended Campbell but after the judgement of the General Assembly the issue died down.

On 27 May 1831 Alexander Scott was charged with heresy for the same reason before the presbytery of Paisley, and deprived of his licence to preach, a sentence which was later confirmed by the General Assembly.

As for Edward Irving, the London Presbytery found him guilty of heresy in November 1830. In April 1832 he was thrown out of the National Scotch Church for allowing laity to lead parts of the service. In March 1833, the Church of Scotland in Irving's hometown of Annan charged him with heresy regarding Irving's doctrine of the "sinfulness of our Lord's human nature." He was inevitably found guilty.

So, all those who were telling truth about the atonement were silenced by the Church of Scotland.

Tongues Revival

As for the main people involved with tongues, prophecy, etc in Scotland, the enemy chose a different way to silence them. I have already described how Mary Campbell fell back towards the world and she died young in 1839. Margaret Macdonald died in 1840 at the age of just twenty-five. Her brothers, James and George both died in 1835 from tuberculosis. They all died so young!

Some visitors to the revival thought that it was a genuine move of God, but many thought it was demonic. It is understandable that there was such opposition because, as I have already mentioned, they had nothing to compare with. We can now look back at what happened with much more knowledge and experience than they did in 1830 and for various reasons I am certain this was a powerful move of God.

(All the quotes above that are not attributed, all come from, 'Memoir of the life of Rev Robert Story' written by his son in 1862)

England

Finally, we turn to London to see what happened there.

Edward Irving was expectant of the spiritual gifts breaking out in his church. After the six returned from Scotland, prayer groups were started in various homes to pray for an outpouring of Holy Spirit. Irving began a 6.30am prayer-meeting in the spring of 1831 where up to a thousand people attended. On April 30th Miss Cardale spoke in tongues and prophesied in a private meeting; the first such occurrence in London. Others started to speak in tongues as well, but the church's board members generally opposed the manifestation of the Gifts and did not want them happening inside the official church meeting. Unfortunately, those who were using tongues wanted them in the Sunday meeting, so Irving had a problem:

"It was not until the end of October did the new wonder manifest itself publicly. In the interval, despite his eagerness and strong fascination in favour of these miraculous occurrences, Irving took the part of an investigator, and, according to his own conviction, examined closely and severely into the wonderful phenomena now presented before him."

In the end the decision was taken out of Irving's hands. A Mr Pilkington testified to what happened in the Sunday service:

"... and was, as usual, much gratified and comforted by Mr Irving's lectures and prayers; but I was very unexpectedly interrupted by the well-known voice of one of the sisters, who, finding she was unable to restrain herself, and respecting the rules of the Church, rushed into the vestry, and gave vent to speaking in tongues; whilst another, as I understood, from the same impulse, ran down the side aisle, and out of the church, through the principal door. The sudden, doleful, and unintelligible sounds, being heard by all the congregation produced the utmost confusion; standing up, trying to hear, see, and understand, by each and every one of perhaps 1,000 or 2,000 persons, created a noise which may be easily conceived. Mr Irving begged for attention, and when order was restored, he explained what happened, which he said was not new, except in the congregation, where he had been for some time considering the suitability of introducing it; but though satisfied of the correctness of such a measure, he was afraid of introducing it to the congregation; nevertheless, as it was now brought forward by God's will, he felt it his duty to submit. He then said he would change the sermon intended for the day, and instead speak on the 14th chapter of Corinthians, in order to clarify what had just happened. The sister was now returning from the vestry to her seat, and Mr Irving, observing her from the pulpit, said, in an affectionate tone, "Console yourself, sister! Console yourself!" He then proceeded with his sermon."

At the evening service, Irving announced that he would allow tongues and prophecies in the meetings and he preached on the Baptism of Holy Spirit at the mid-week meetings. The board of trustees were against the exercising of these gifts as they thought the service became disorderly. The board brought the issue before the London Presbytery, who, in May 1832 decided Irving was in violation of the order of worship and he was locked out of the church. As a result, Irving took nearly all his congregation to a new building in Newman Street, London.

Irving had long believed and preached on the imminent second coming of Christ. He and his congregation were convinced that this was going to happen. In their new independent church, they set up a new government based upon Church authority resting on the apostles. In November they appointed John Cardale as the first apostle. They appointed prophets, elders, evangelists and deacons and gave Irving the title of 'angel'. Irving taught on the restoration of the Gifts, the Baptism of Holy Spirit and Healing.

Irving wrote several theological papers including the subject of supernatural gifts etc. After Irving was kicked out of the Church of Scotland in March 1833. his influence in his church declined, but sadly he had something more important to worry about, his health. He was showing signs of tuberculosis and he died at the end of 1834.

(The quotations above came from, The Life of Edward Irving, Volume 2 by Mrs Oliphants 1862)

In 1832 Henry Drummond formed his own 'church' down at Albury. A few months later one of them spoke in tongues and prophesied. Drummond began speaking in tongues and prophesied and by 1834 the church was two hundred strong. Newman Street, London and Albury were both part of the Catholic Apostolic Church as they called themselves in 1849. Albury became the centre of government for the new organisation. All appointments and major decisions were made through prophecy. The Catholic Apostolic Church pretty well died out in the 20th century.

Clearly the Spiritual Gifts were exercised in the Catholic Apostolic Church after Irving's death, but I have not been able to trace them any further. It would be interesting to know if they continued with the Gifts into the twentieth century, therefore being a link to the outbreak of Pentecostalism.

Conclusion

So, that was the end of the revival. As far as my research goes to date, it was also the end of the manifestation of the Gifts of the Spirit in the United Kingdom, in a public setting, for many years. I am sure individuals spoke in tongues, prophesied and were involved in healing, but I am unaware of this being widespread.

The first teaching and practicing of healing seems to have been through William Boardman, who put on a Healing conference in 1885, at which many Europeans and even Americans participated. Tongues became widely practiced after the 1906 Azusa Street revival in Los Angeles. However, it was not until the 1980s that Prophecy became widely taught and used.

In my opinion the enemy stopped us widely using the Gifts of the Spirit for a very long time.

I find this revival a fascinating and key part of our spiritual history and we can learn from it going forward. When the Lord gives new revelation, the gift of discernment is critically important. Time and again we see something new being rejected by the Church, instead of discernment being exercised and a recognition of what was from the Lord and what was not.

Unfortunately, denominations seem to build traditions around themselves that make them oppose anything new. The Methodist Church, in its early days rejected camp meetings where revival was breaking out regularly and threw two people out of the church who wanted to pursue them. The result was a church split and the creation of the Primitive Methodists. This was less than twenty years after Wesley's death, and they rejected these outdoor revival meetings which were the foundation of Wesley's ministry in the 1730s.

During any move of God, and whenever we are in front line ministry, we must be watchful because there will likely be persecution and attacks from the enemy, from people and the church.

Chapter Four

The 1858-64 Revival

How many of you have heard of the 1859 revival that went across the whole of the United Kingdom and was the largest revival we have ever known?

It is strange that it is so unknown, especially as it was the most widely reported in UK history. It is a big subject, so I am going to break the story down by country, first Ulster as it was there that the revival first appeared in the United Kingdom.

ULSTER

Ulster is not an often-used term, but it is made up of the six counties of Northern Ireland plus Cavan, Donegal and Monaghan in Ireland.

The different counties of Ulster were religiously different with some mainly Protestant, some predominantly Presbyterian and other counties mainly Catholic. By 1859 the Presbyterian church had settled into generally Orthodox teaching. There was a deadness as far as spiritual power was concerned, most could be described as nominal Christians, there being form but little substance. However, amongst the ministers there was a desire to see the Church refreshed by a move of God.

The beginning of this story can be marked as a lesson to all of us. In the Spring of 1856, an English evangelist, Mrs Colville, came to Ballymena to go house to house with the

The 1858-64 Revival

Gospel message. She went away quite depressed because of the little fruit she perceived came from her hard work. However, she came to a house in Mill Street on November 3rd, where there were a few young ladies and a young man, James McQuilkin. During a conversation with one of the ladies about her spiritual condition, Mrs Colville said, "My dear, you have never known the Lord Jesus". McQuilkin felt these words referred to him and they were like a dagger to his heart. After weeks of wrestling with conviction, he gave his life to Jesus.

James McQuilkin began to testify about his new-found Saviour and his friends saw the change in his life as he put aside worldly activities. He had a long conversation with Jeremiah Meneely and later testified to two more of his friends, Robert Carlisle and John Wallace. All three became born again and in September 1857 the four friends decided to pray every Friday in the old schoolhouse for God's blessings on their activities. McQuilkin was inspired by reading how God answered George Muller's prayers.

During that same month, Jeremiah Lamphier began a prayer meeting in New York, which led, almost immediately to an awakening that brought about one million souls into the Kingdom of God.

The friends had one great object; they were praying for an outpouring of the Holy Spirit upon themselves and upon the surrounding country. On New Year's Day 1858 the young prayers were encouraged by a farm servant being converted and another young man found Jesus and joined their group. They were also inspired by the news coming from America. These early meetings consisted of reading the Bible, prayer and meditation and people were converted every night they met. By the end of the year 1858 about fifty young men were taking part in the prayer meeting. This prayer meeting was to start the biggest revival the UK had seen – so far!

It is strange that everybody talks about the 1859 Ulster Revival when the Spirit of God was clearly working in the area in 1858. One of the original four members of the prayer meeting said:

> "The work was confined to this parish (Connor) during the year 1858. Beside the regular prayer meeting for Christian men only we had cottage meetings until no cottage was large enough to hold the people. We also had great open-air meetings."

As the news spread the four were in great demand by those who wanted to know what God was doing.

A convert from a meeting in the Connor district, returned home at Christmas time to Ahoghill. He read the Bible and prayed with his family so powerfully that that night his mother was crying out for mercy. His mother and sister came to the Lord that night. He returned for another visit and another family came to Christ. As a result, James McQuilkin and two original members of his group held a meeting in the Second Presbyterian Church of Ahoghill on February 2nd, 1859 and another two weeks later; interest began to stir in the area.

On March 14th saw a meeting was held at the First Presbyterian Church and it was so packed they had to stop it for fear of the galleries falling down. A layman addressed three thousand people outside in the chilling rain and hundreds fell on their knees in the mud. Seven hundred were awakened and the two other Presbyterian churches in the town were crowded out. People's lives were transformed from every level of society and across different denominations. Many were 'prostrated' under deep conviction of sin which caused quite a lot of controversy.

Twelve days later, Ballymena, just three miles away, was impacted. Many came under deep conviction and a group of young laymen spent most of their time helping the people to find their way to Jesus.

"The awakening spread with the rapidity of a wildfire when it is fanned with a mighty breeze." Within four months the revival was all over Ulster. Often the fire started through the testimony of young people who were visiting from revival areas.

The areas where it was most intense were in Protestant areas. County Antrim was significantly impacted by the revival being 54% Presbyterian, 18% Episcopalian and only 25% Catholic. But County Fermanagh was not so impacted being 2% Presbyterian, 38% Episcopalian and 56% Catholic.

Ulster suffered a great deal from sectarianism; there being great antipathy between the Protestants and Catholics. The Catholics were generally very opposed to the revival. One bishop said that people who were influenced by the devil were taking Bibles around to ruin the people. Some violently attacked evangelical ministers and their priests would sell Holy Water to counter the 'revival devil' and instructed their people to boycott the revival meetings. This did not stop some going and several hundred were touched by God and became Protestants. There was a significant cost to pay for some of the converts as they were ejected from their families and received other persecution such as beatings.

As the revival progressed some of the priests recognised the good that was being done and in fact there was a significant decline in sectarianism. This was largely due to various Protestants going to Catholics and asking for forgiveness for the way they had treated them. Sadly, this peace did not last.

WALES

Wales had experienced many, many revivals over the previous 120 years, but the people had become lukewarm in the years prior to 1859. Preaching had become very intellectual and theatrical - again a lot of form but little substance. There was a longing by the older generation to experience a revival again.

The revival began through two men, David Morgan, a 45 year old Calvinistic Methodist and Humphrey Jones, a 27 year old Wesleyan Methodist.

Jones was a revivalist who emigrated to the United States in 1854 where he got involved in the Jeremiah Lamphier revival of 1857. In 1858 he returned to Wales, bringing with him something of the revival. From July to September, he held missions in towns near to where he lived. The meetings were particularly fruitful. In September, he held a mission at Pontrhydygroes where he met David Morgan.

Morgan had been praying for revival for ten years by the time he heard about these powerful meetings, but being a Wesleyan and not a Calvinistic Methodist he was a bit suspicious about them. Nevertheless, he went to a meeting and was very troubled by the message of 'not being hot or cold'. He was unable to sleep so he went to see Jones where he was staying. Jones had asked the Lord for someone to work with and he heard the Lord say that Morgan was the man. It was agreed that he would preach in Morgan's church that Sunday in Ysbytty, Gwynedd.

Humphrey Jones spoke on 'Woe to them that are at ease in Zion' to try to stir up the church members to action. After the service he complained about the coldness of the people and that nobody even gave an 'Amen'. An elder stood up to say that it was difficult to say 'Amen' under a ministry that he felt was condemning him. A witness said:

"As he said those words he almost fainted back into his seat. At that moment something went through the whole congregation until everyone put down his head and wept!... the following week men came in crowds from the mountains and all the country around until we were afraid the chapel would come down."

Morgan had been seeking more power in his preaching for some time now, but particularly so over this week. He wrote that on the Tuesday night, "I awoke about four in the morning, remembering everything of a religious nature I had ever learnt or heard." This was the first of several God encounters he experienced over the coming months. He said at the end of the year, "I have been wrestling for the blessing, and I have received it."

I believe this was the Baptism of Fire he received. He then ministered in the power of the Holy Spirit for the next two years, then amazingly he woke up one morning and he knew the power had left him and it never returned. I have never come across anything like this before. Can you imagine being used by God so powerfully all around your nation and then having the power removed?

At first David Morgan did not like the way Jones ministered, but he saw how powerful the results were, so he adopted it himself. He would preach the gospel first, then he would come down from the pulpit and give a fiery message to the unsaved. He would then say that there was going to be a meeting of church members and anyone who wanted to give their lives to the Lord – everyone else had to leave. The converted would stay behind and Morgan would call them forward and speak to each one trying to find out their spiritual condition in order to give them a corrective word if required. Then he would kneel and commend each of the converts by name to God and welcome them into the church.

The 1858-64 Revival

By the middle of November 1859, the revivalists decided to go their separate ways and very sadly in December it became apparent that there was something wrong with Humphrey Jones mentally. He gave up ministry for several years, then started again. In 1871 he returned to America where he died in 1895.

By the end of the year there were over two hundred converts in the area that had a population of less than one thousand.

An example of one of Morgan's meetings. David Morgan and his friend were approached by two elders from a country area to hold a service the following day. Morgan felt it was of the Lord so he said he could fit it in at 8:00am. The elders rushed home and went all over the moors and hillside to tell people there was to be a meeting:

> "The chapel was crowded with worshippers at eight. We had only taken hold of the hymn-book when the elders were melted into tears; and before the hymn was all read, the weeping had spread to the congregation. Both young men and girls, old men and children, and mothers in Israel wept unrestrainedly. Stalwart farmhands were struck down by the mere reading of the hymn. God filled the place! At the close of the service only nine came forward to give their lives to the Lord, but the arrows of truth had transfixed many others, who left the service literally shrieking with mental anguish. They could be heard screaming in paroxysms of agony as they climbed the hills in the distance towards their homes. When the preachers were getting on their horses, a man came to them, shaking with sobs, and said, 'I went out this morning, but I have decided to join the society tomorrow.' Before they had proceeded a hundred yards, a husband and wife with tear-stained cheeks

hailed them, and said, 'We turned our backs just now on Christ, but we will give ourselves to God's people tomorrow.' Stranger than the service, was to see people crossing the fields in ones and twos to meet us, and all telling us the same story that they were going to join the church tomorrow."

The revival spread throughout Wales. For a while David Morgan concentrated on the Ceredigion area before moving around the country. For about two years he was used very powerfully. Previous revivals had been led by great leaders, but this one seems to have spread mainly through prayer meetings.

SCOTLAND

Spiritually Scotland does not seem to have been too bad immediately prior to the 1858 revival, although, as in Ulster and Wales a lot of the preaching was form over substance. There were few revivals in the fifteen years leading up to this one, but there does seem to have been a certain vigour within the Church. This may have been as a result of a third of the Church of Scotland leaving to set up the Free Church in 1843. This perceived new-found freedom probably gave strength to many of their ministries.

Like the rest of the United Kingdom many ministers in Scotland were aware of the revival that was going on in the USA and they were very encouraged when getting regular news, believing that whatever happened there could happen in their nation. The first action was generally to set up a prayer meeting to pray in the revival. A number of people around Scotland were praying and expectant for God to do something.

A prelude to the revival was the relatively new concept of lay preachers. Brownlow North and Hay Macdowall Grant were two such men and they did successful preaching tours in different parts of Scotland in 1857 and 1858. The Lord used them to break up the dry ground to make people more receptive to what was to come.

So, with that backdrop the Lord sent Brownlow North and an experienced English evangelist, Reginald Radcliffe to Aberdeen at the same time. North had quite a reputation in Scotland, so his meetings were immediately packed and there were stirring results. However, Radcliffe was unknown, so he had to take a different approach.

At the invitation of a professor at Marischal College, Radcliffe arrived in Aberdeen on the 27th November 1858, as the revival was just starting in Ulster and Wales. Despite antagonism from ministers, particularly Church of Scotland ministers, towards lay preachers, he started meetings in a Mission room. (It would be a further six months before the Church of Scotland approved lay ministers speaking in their churches.) As the ministers had no problem if it was the children who were spoken to, Radcliffe started with the children. Immediately the Spirit of God joined in and many of the children sought salvation. This made their parents wonder what was going on, so they joined the meetings.

Holy Spirit was moving so powerfully that Radcliffe wrote in his first week in Aberdeen, "I believe great things are in store for our land." He had planned to stay ten days, but he ended up staying five months. Scores of children received salvation and prayer meetings were started all over the city.

On seeing Holy Spirit at work some Free Church ministers joined in. Foremost among the supporters was James Smith, the Church of Scotland minister at Greyfriars Parish Church who invited Radcliffe to speak. This caused an uproar amongst many of the churches in Aberdeen as they did not approve of lay preachers preaching on Sunday. He was sensitive to these concerns, so he did not preach from the pulpit. Radcliffe got into some churches because he was speaking mainly to children.

The movement increased very quickly with Radcliffe conducting up to thirty meetings per week, including seven on Sundays. No sooner had one service closed than people poured in for the next. In order to placate the opposition, North and Radcliffe had to say they were giving 'addresses' on their leaflets and posters. North left after two weeks and Radcliffe soldiered on – the pace was exhausting.

Radcliffe understood that to succeed he had to be humble so that Holy Spirit could use him to the maximum. At the end of 1858 he wrote "I tremble here on the edge of a great work... I want to lie in the dust and be guided from on high". He wanted the flame to go around Scotland and then around the world through ports like Aberdeen. He did not have a strategy to evangelise the nation, he just kept listening to what 'the Captain' said.

By early February no building was big enough. To make a comparison, by now in Ulster and Wales the revival had begun to spread out from where it initially started. Also, at this time the Church of Scotland local Presbytery met and almost removed the Greyfriar's minister for hosting Radcliffe.

The controversy just attracted bigger crowds and the constant workload on Radcliffe had its effect. On March 19th 1859, his health broke down and he went away to rest for several months, handing over the work to others.

The revival then burst out in several areas in July, including Glasgow. I am not entirely sure why there was a gap of several months before the revival really started to get going in Scotland. It could be something to do with the large numbers of ministers who went to experience the revival in Ulster and then brought it back home. But once the fires began, they spread with varying intensity around Scotland over the next two years.

The places most impacted by the revival were the major cities of Glasgow, Dundee, Aberdeen and the whole of Aberdeenshire. It was said that scarcely anywhere between Aberdeen and Inverness was not touched by the revival. It was particularly fierce in the fishing villages between Fraserburgh and Nairn. It went along the river Spey, the whole of Perthshire, around Montrose on the East Coast and further south between Eyemouth and Dunbar. Port Glasgow, Greenock, Ayrshire and nearly every village and town in Dumfriesshire was touched. The Inner and Outer Hebrides, the Orkneys and Shetlands were also impacted, which means most of Scotland was impacted.
The only places that seemed to largely miss out were Rosshire and Sutherland, possibly due to their antagonism to lay preaching.

ENGLAND

The start of the revival in England is much more difficult to relate as there does not seem to be a clear story here. The other three countries have very clear beginnings, but virtually nobody seems to have written about the revival in England.

Edwin Orr's book, 'The Second Evangelical Awakening in Britain' written in 1949, had as his main source the eight page 'The Revival' weekly newspaper began in July 1859 in order to record the revival in the UK. It simply did not have the room to publish all the revival accounts it was.

There were only about twenty places in England touched by the revival in the last four months of 1859, and most were ignited by regular prayer or by testimony about what was going on in America or Ulster. The light that seemed to start the fire, particularly in London, was the worldwide prayer meeting that took place in the second week of 1860.

London had 2.8 million people living there, which was nearly seven times larger than the two next biggest cities of Glasgow and Liverpool.

As in other parts of the UK, people started united prayer meetings on hearing the revival news from different areas. In London, daily meetings were organised in Crosby Hall in September 1859 and by the end of the year there were 120 prayer meetings in London, a quarter of them daily, the rest weekly. The numbers grew until it was better to ask where there was not a prayer meeting. The movement was unprecedented.

Unlike anywhere else people got together to plan how to reach the vast numbers in London. One of the most successful ideas was to hire theatres and halls to hold meetings for the workers and the poor during the winter season; people who generally had never set foot in a church before. This was only possible because the Earl of Shaftesbury had promoted a bill four years earlier that allowed Christian meetings in un-consecrated buildings.

At the beginning of 1860 he formed a committee and by the end of February they hired seven theatres where 20,000 people heard the gospel every Sunday. For the upper and middle classes, St Paul's, Westminster Abbey and two halls were hired in the West End. Seeing how successful these meetings were, others hired halls and theatres across London, until there were about twenty venues being used and an estimated million people heard the gospel during the season.

The 1858-64 Revival

These Sunday services were led by travelling revivalists such as the amazing Reginald Radcliffe and Richard Weaver. Wherever they went the venues could not hold the numbers who wanted to get in and many gave their lives to Jesus in each service. Although testimonies were often given during the services, they were dominated by preaching.

As well as these large general meetings there were initiatives all over London to reach different groups. One of the best was the midnight meetings that were held monthly for prostitutes. A team would go onto the streets and offer invitations to the women to come to the meeting. They normally had 150-300 attend and in the first year there were 19 meetings where 4,000 attended, 23,000 tracts were given out. 89 women returned home; 75 found other jobs; 6 got married; 81 moved into refuges, and others were helped out of the business. This movement spread and it is estimated that 1,000 prostitutes were rescued.

Another group went in twos in carriages to different streets – they would get out and preach the gospel before riding to another street; when it rained they visited homes and then held meetings in the evenings. Another group held special meetings for lamplighters, and another for one thousand people while they picked hops.

My favourite was a man called boatswain Smith, who took a boat out into the port among other boats, blew his boatswain's whistle, attracting the sailors' attention and then he preached the gospel from his little boat. People held meetings in schools, hospitals, parks, factories and orphanages – just about anywhere where there were unsaved people.

It is not known how many were saved in London, but clearly a great proportion were reached with the gospel. One person wrote:

"There must be a great deal of good doing in London, for one can hardly pass the end of a street of a fine evening or of a Sunday, without hearing someone preaching and not only men but women."

Although there are many accounts of revival in England, I do not get the feeling of the country being on fire, as I do with the other three countries. I have spent some time puzzling over this and have come up with the following thoughts. Ulster and Wales in particular are tiny countries, so it is likely that the news of what was going on in different areas would have been spread very quickly and compared to England, the other three countries had hardly any large cities, only Glasgow, Edinburgh and Belfast were over 100,000.

This meant that they were made up mostly of small towns and villages where communities were much more prevalent. In communities people congregate together and they know each other well, so when someone gives their life to the Lord they are aware of that person's history and they have an understanding of the true miracle that has taken place when their friend's life is turned around. Revival is therefore likely to burn through the whole community.

It does not appear that the other English cities received the same attention as London. Radcliffe hired halls in Liverpool in the autumn of 1861 – in fact the revival only really got going in Manchester and Liverpool at that time. I cannot find much for Birmingham, Leeds and Sheffield, but Bristol seems to have been very active in the revival.

Around the country the Revival newspaper was often read out to encourage people and fires were lit through the testimonies in it. It seems that the major revivalists such as Radcliffe and Weaver were used to break through. They almost always had wonderful meetings and when they left the area local evangelists came in to build on what had been started.

One group of evangelists were the Woolwich Boys. They were from a boys' refuge and several were saved in 1859. Groups of them were invited to speak all around the country and many a fire was lit by their testimonies.

Radcliffe was constantly calling for more evangelists; undoubtedly there would have been more saved in England had there been more workers.

CHARACTERISTICS OF REVIVAL

I will compare the main characteristics of the revival as they relate across the four countries.

Unity

Unity was a characteristic of the revival everywhere and was crucial for its success as the Lord blesses unity. Apart from unity between denominations, there was also unity within denominations. It was also about unity in communities and in Ulster there was a great coming together between the Protestant and Catholic communities.

I believe that part of the reason why the revival was so successful in Ulster and Wales was because the Protestant church was the dominating denomination - Presbyterian and Calvinistic Methodist - and they fully supported the revival. Instructions on how to organise prayer meetings and support revival efforts really helped spread the fire widely and deeply.

England on the other hand was dominated by the Church of England which is seldom united behind anything and England also had multiple denominations to deal with which made unity that much more difficult to achieve.

Prayer

A prayer meeting birthed the revival. Some ministers who were unhappy with the spiritual state of their churches had begun prayer meetings in 1858 to pray revival in, particularly in Wales. Many more began praying on the news of what was happening in the USA and Ulster. This helped birth the revival all over the United Kingdom and thousands more people sustained it. Whereas testimony was the main means of spreading the revival in Ulster, in Wales it was prayer:

> "I am persuaded that the means blessed of God to create and carry on the revival in most places, if not in ALL, is PRAYER. You can trace its origin and progress in every locality, to prayer, especially the prayers of the new converts."

> "More, boats' crews have come to shore in a converted state. The Spirit has come upon them while at sea, and they have knelt in prayer at the bottom of the boats."

> "It is prayer - prevailing, believing, wrestling prayer, which is the secret of all success."

> "In a town of 9,000, 4,000 people were in prayer meetings on a weeknight."

> "It is not unusual to see thousands assembled for prayer in a graveyard or a large gravel pit."

Prayer was so infectious it was as if Holy Spirit jumped from one person to another like a holy virus. I believe that Holy Spirit was hovering over the whole of the United Kingdom at this time. When the people came together for a prayer meeting, beseeching God for the revival rains to fall, they were opening themselves up to receive Holy

Spirit. He responded by releasing the revival fires through these people.

It was not just corporate prayer meetings that spread the revival. In most places the reaction of the people to what Holy Spirit was doing, was to go home and start daily family meetings. In some villages almost every home had family meetings:

> "A prayer meeting was said to have existed in almost every second house…"

> "Prior to the revival, only three houses conducted family worship out of 30, but afterwards only three didn't."

These prayers were mainly travailing prayers, pulling heaven down to earth. However, I have discovered that a 'spirit of prayer' prevailed across the United Kingdom:

> "We have been greatly struck by the fact that so much of the spirit of prayer has possessed the Lord's people. They draw the heaven of heavens, as it were, into every prayer meeting; such congregations as were never before seen are brought to¬gether on these occasions. But, in every one of them, there is something more than a large congregation - the prayers penetrate the hearts of those who attend, whether they be male or female, even persons who scarcely attended a place of worship are impressed."

> "Prayer meetings, attended by hundreds, are most efficiently conducted by the converts, and then such prayers! So earnest - so scriptural - prayers like those of the old Puritans, which go up like red-hot bolts to heaven."

Physical Manifestations

These were much more of a characteristic of the Ulster revival. There were some localised manifestations in Scotland, mainly where Ulstermen ministered, but virtually none in Wales or England.

We are much more used to them these days, but in 1859 there was a lot of controversy over manifestations as the Church always wanted everything to be 'in order'. However, those at the centre of the revival recognised that these were mostly of the Holy Spirit and in fact some leaders recognised that some of the unsaved were impacted positively by seeing the Holy Spirit at work.

Interesting that these days some church leaders think it important to have 'Seeker Sensitive' services as they think Holy Spirit puts off the unsaved!

The manifestations were only on the minority of people, but of course they were highlighted by the newspapers; they lessened as time went on.

Testimony

The one thing that stands out from the many reports on the revival in Ulster is that for the majority of towns the revival began through TESTIMONY! The word testimony in Hebrew means **'do it again Lord in the same power and authority'**. So, every time you testify you are asking the Lord to do it again. This is really powerful! What touched off the revival in many places was laymen testifying to what had happened in their town and while testifying Holy Spirit fell:

> "Next evening we met again in the open air. A gentleman addressed the assembled throng. He recounted the scenes he had witnessed in

the neighbourhood he had just left. The people listened with wonder, humility, and awe. As they were about to separate, one fell to the ground screaming for mercy, then another, and another, till the fallen ones might have been counted by scores! Multitudes remained till the morning light, alternately engaged in singing and prayer."

A different type of testimony:

"The girl who had found peace on the previous Sabbath evening stood up, declared that she was happy in the Lord, and simply added the words, 'Come to Jesus.' The effect of her invitation was like the effect of an electric shock, and many sinners came that evening, weary and heavy-laden, to Jesus, and found rest for their souls."

Another example:

"The Spirit was preparing the soil for a special shower of blessing, and that morning a little girl came into the girls' school, and with joy sparkling in her eyes she threw up her arms and exclaimed, 'I have found Jesus!' Instantly, an electric sympathy ran from heart to heart, and a large number of the children fell down on their knees weeping over their sinfulness and crying to the Saviour for mercy. Some of them were heard before long, pleading with their parents to repent and turn to God."

The new converts were themselves a testimony: "The worshipful, joyous solemnity that appears on the faces of the converts is truly heavenly and generally has a strange and thrilling effect on mere onlookers."

Lay Evangelists

This revival was the first to be spread in a significant way by itinerant evangelists. Apart from David Morgan, these were not used much in Wales. Some were used in Ulster, but a lot in Scotland and England.

Some were known as 'Gentlemen preachers' such as Brownlow North and Reginald Radcliffe, together with Hay Macdowall Grant and others. Then there were the Americans – Phoebe Palmer, Charles Finney and E P Hammond who was particularly successful in the southwest of Scotland and amongst children. Finally, there were the evangelists who related to the masses such as the collier Richard Weaver and the chimney sweep William Carter.

Reginald Radcliffe had an unusual way of preaching in that he spoke very simply, and he only spoke for about twenty minutes. One man was not hugely expectant when he went to one of Radcliffe's meetings as he was anything but impressed with his preaching. However, he had to earnestly repent when he saw the fruit that came from it.

Brownlow North spent three hours with the Lord every morning and I suspect most of them did the same. Radcliffe also spent a lot of time with God:

> "Some truth would grab hold of him and when the meeting was held he poured it out like a torrent of lava; attacking the conscience, awakening the sleeper, terrifying the careless and in the bright light of the Spirit revealing the Lamb of God"

The amount of work this revival generated was so much that the health of several of them broke down and they had to take several months rest. Brownlow North, who was a forerunner to the revival, had to take three years off at the revival's peak. As an example of how hard they worked, Macdowall Grant spoke to 2,031 people individually about salvation and preached fifty-five times in fifty days.

New converts were in effect lay evangelists as well. In Ulster, young converts would walk down the road and tell of their experiences to people in the next village – the Glory of God would fall and the revival began there. Parents would become evangelists to their children and indeed children to their parents. Basically, as soon as many of the people were converted, they started evangelising.

Conversion

This revival is a very clear example of how people were saved through conviction of sin. They were first convicted by Holy Spirit of how sinful they were; some would actually see visions of hell and scream out in fear. At that point people would gather around to point the person to Christ. They would then be awakened to the fact that Jesus was the answer and would often cry for mercy and ask, 'what must I do to be saved?'

After a period, which could be a few minutes or a few days or a few months, they would find peace through realising that, by faith, their sins had been forgiven and they would then be filled with joy. This has been the process in every revival except the 1904 Welsh revival where love was preached.

Someone observed:

> "For many their soul is in danger, on the brink of, almost IN hell. They see it, they feel it and in deep mental distress cry for deliverance. A Saviour is revealed to them in their despair; they behold Him; believe in Him; they are rescued, saved and they know it. They rejoice and leap for joy!"

This is what people generally experienced during the services or indeed just after they went outside.

Here are a few descriptions of meetings:

> "One of the converts said a few things to the people, then here and there throughout the church, parties rose and went out, labouring under deep conviction, and immediately the graveyard is filled with groups singing and praying around the prostrate bodies of men and women. Some are as in a trance, others crying for mercy. Some are still falling into the arms of friends and sinking as into a faint and a few rush to the gates and fly in terror from the scene."

> "The scene when we arrived baffles all description. Imagine a large meadow, with an immense multitude of people in all attitudes — some praying, weeping and crying for mercy, others lying in utter helplessness only able to utter feebly their entreaties for pardon, surrounded by groups of friends and strangers all interceding for them and urging them on to call on Christ and, again, others with their faces gleaming with a more than earthly light, listening to the speaker in ecstasy or eyes raised, eloquently praising God."

> "While one of these, a lad of fourteen, gave an account of his conversion, and, with tears, entreated the people to come to the Saviour, another lad began to sob and weep. The young convert then ran forward, caught the penitent in his arms, and besought him to look to Jesus, and he would be saved. The affection of the boy seemed to break down the hearts of the people; one general cry burst forth from the congregation, and sinners fell all around, confessing their sins and imploring

pardon. The saved of the Lord were many, and they were but the first fruits of a glorious harvest."

"In a moment, as if struck with a thunderbolt, about a hundred people were prostrated on their knees, issuing a wail from hearts bruised, broken, and overwhelmed with horror, such as will never be forgotten."

"Persons of every shade of temperament and character were mysteriously affected, overpowered, prostrated, and made to pour out the most thrilling agonising cries for mercy. Most of those impressed and awakened found peace and comfort in a very short space of time, and then their faces shone with a sweetness and glory beyond description. Very many of them received a marvellous fluency and power of prayer. A hatred of sin, a love for the Saviour, a zeal for His cause, affection for one another, and an anxiety about perishing sinners, took absolute possession of their hearts, and literally ruled and governed their actions."

The itinerant revivalists brought something new. Reginald Radcliffe preached that salvation could be received immediately, there and then. This caused concern with some ministers, especially those in Scotland who preferred that people be on trial for months to ensure they were properly converted.

Radcliffe and others would often preach to the converted in a meeting first and then preach to the unconverted. They would then take those people who were interested in salvation to another room where they or others would have a conversation with each person, pointing them to Jesus.

Radcliffe said that he believed about two-thirds of conversions came as a result of the conversation and one-third through preaching. Phoebe Palmer, the American revivalist introduced the 'penitent form', calling people forward to a rail if they wanted salvation. Over time this changed until Billy Graham started the 'altar call'.

Trains

Only a few years before the revival started, trains had been introduced to the north of Scotland and other parts of the United Kingdom. This was the first revival where trains were used for hungry people to get to meetings and for revivalists to travel to speaking engagements. They enabled people like Radcliffe to leave Scotland and travel down to London for a few meetings before quickly returning.

Travelling to see what was going on in Ulster was much easier due to trains. Many ministers visited Ulster, particularly from Scotland and either brought the revival atmosphere back with them or their expectancy that God would move was heightened significantly.

Children

Large numbers of young, even as young as eight years old, were impacted all over the United Kingdom by this awakening and took part in it:

> "One of the most striking characteristics of this move¬ment is its effects on young people, and even on children. The youth of our congregations are nearly all the subjects of deep religious impressions. Many of them seem as if filled with the spirit of prayer. Very young people, even children from ten to fourteen, gather together to hold prayer meetings and pray very fervently."

The Word

Humphrey Jones wrote:

> "Two things are necessary to be a successful preacher: first to pray much in secret – to be there many times in the day, wrestling with God – to wrestle each time as if it were the last, and not to rise from your knees until you have a proof that the Lord has heard you. Ask the Lord in faith and with great fervency, what to say to the people. Go straight from your closet to the pulpit each time, then the anointing will follow your preaching. Another thing is to preach pointedly and rousingly – aiming at the conscience each time – telling people their sins to their faces. I would wish to preach each time as if I had to die in the pulpit when I had done preaching – as if I had to go direct from the pulpit to judgement."

How many preachers do this today?

The Word was king in this revival, especially in Wales; unlike in the 1904 Welsh revival.

Someone else wrote:

> "There was a beauty, a loveliness about the Holy Word which we had never before perceived. New light seemed to be thrown upon it. It electrified us and caused us to weep with joy! The feeling became general. All present were under its influence. The hardest hearts were forced to succumb. And then we sang, sang with spirit and repeated the hymn again and again - we could not leave off. Every heart seemed inspired to continue and the last two lines were sung for a full quarter of an hour. Then the minister prayed and such a prayer we had never

before heard spoken. We felt we were communing with God. We could have prayed all night. The meeting lasted four hours."

The Bible was read out loud in the streets, particularly in London and the Word was preached all over the United Kingdom, in churches, factories, theatres – everywhere! Huge numbers of Bibles were sold to the hungry converts.

Hymns

As with most large revivals, this one had its own form of hymns. Richard Weaver published his own book of songs. These were quite a different style to the old hymns and caused a reaction among some ministers in Scotland, however, they were very popular with many in England and Scotland.

Some songs became particularly popular. I discovered that one with a refrain of 'Christ for me! Christ for me!' led a number of people to Jesus. One person heard Weaver singing it and went into the meeting and at the end of the service, after having given her life to Christ, gave Weaver a rope with which she was going to tie her legs before throwing herself off a bridge!

Open Air Meetings

All over the Kingdom, many tens of thousands went to large meetings during the summer.

Sadly today the summer events that do still happen are only for Christians with no evangelistic impact on people or communities

Tracts

Handing out of tracts was very common and their impact

on individuals was sometimes considerable. This was a popular form of evangelism even before the revival, but hundreds of thousands, if not millions were given out in these revival times.

REVIVAL FRUIT

Transformation

Ministers seem to have been absolutely amazed at what went on in their area. The extraordinary number of people who were being born again, the rapt attention they all had from their congregations, the transformation of the lives of those who had been touched by God.

One person wrote that:

> "The spirit of these newly awakened persons is all gentleness, teachableness, and humility, while the fruits of the Spirit - love, joy, peace - rule in their hearts most clearly."

Streets that had been dangerous to walk in were now peaceful, prostitutes, drunkards and crooks were giving their lives to Jesus. Some said that there was someone converted in most of the houses in their area; they could walk through their parish and hear worship and prayer coming from many of the houses. Lives were transformed, entire neighbourhoods were transformed.

Here are some more testimonies:

> "This was the most degraded of Irish villages. Rioting and drunkenness were the order of each evening. Profane swearing and Sabbath desecration were most fashionable sins, and such a place for lying and stealing I do not know. Many a time I longed to get out of it. Well, we have a change now that

is truly gratifying. As you pass down the street you hear, in almost every house, the voice of joy and melody. Stop in the street; name the Name of Jesus, and old and young crowd around you. Raise the voice in praise or prayer and every building pours out its inhabitants to join the company of anxious hearers."

"I found the town in a state of great excitement; many families had not gone to bed for the two or three previous nights. From dozens of houses, night and day, you would hear when passing along, loud cries for mercy from persons under conviction, or the voice of prayer by kind visitors, or the sweet soothing tones of sacred song; business seemed at a standstill. In some streets, four or five groups of people, in houses, and before the open doors and open windows, engaged in prayer or in praise, all at the same time."

"Almost all the miners used to be drunkards. They would come to their work on Monday with bruised faces and blackeyes. The change is above anything I ever knew. There is no company without its prayer meeting underground before starting work. They sing beautifully. On Saturday they gather underground to give thanks for the mercies of the week. There is scarcely a house without its family altar."

Drunkenness was probably the greatest evil of its day and because of this many revival meetings were linked to temperance and the temperance movement grew substantially during this period. When you realise that 15% of all deaths in England at the time were due to drink, you can see the scale of the problem. It is a problem that had been around for hundreds of years because people drank beer/alcohol as water quality was very poor. As a result of many publicans coming to the Lord and the fact that so many conversions took away so much of their business, many pubs closed.

I might suggest that drinking is still a problem today though the water quality is no longer to blame:

> "In Campbeltown, the twenty public houses in that town had only sold seven gills (28 fluid ounces) of whisky during the whole evening among them; such a marked change had come over the people in the habit of frequenting these places."

There was a great change in morality amongst the people – apart from less drinking, there was less swearing, gambling, fighting, etc:

> "The whole morals of the district seem to have undergone a complete change and the police told me that their office was, so far as serious crimes were concerned, all but a sinecure...the minds of the whole community have become impressed and awed by a sense of Divine things."

"One Sabbath evening, after a sermon which was preached by a good man at the entrance to a lane of very bad reputation, a considerable number of prostitutes came out of their houses and marched in a body to the Ulster Penitentiary for the Reform of Fallen Women."

As mentioned, during this period there was a reduction in crime. The Justice of the Peace of one town said there was not 1/10th of the usual number of cases over the previous four months:

> "There appears far less poverty, and even less sickness and death, than ever before. It was reported that drunkenness, swearing and Sabbath

were all but annihilated – the local policeman said that formerly this was the worst wee place in the world."

Long Lasting Fruit

In Wales there was a concern amongst church leaders that those who were being saved in the revival would relapse, so ministers were urged by their Associations to look after the converts through teaching and pastoring them – not easy in revival. Converts were taught that they were not converted unless they had a hatred of sin, a love of holiness, and the exercise of every moral duty. Rigid examination of their spiritual experience, plus training them, led to solid fruit.

Someone did research forty years later and found out that 95% of the converts in Wales stayed the course. Converts across this revival generally, stayed the course well.

Love

The love of Christ overflowed from the hearts of the converted and churchgoers alike. It is very noticeable that generosity to the poor increased substantially. In London particularly, the poor were helped both in spiritual and earthly matters. Philanthropy increased during the revival and for a long time afterwards. Many Christian societies were formed to carry out this work, both in the United Kingdom and abroad.

A few years later, one of these became the Salvation Army and the influential Keswick Convention was born in the revival. The Barnardo homes and many more influential bodies, that did a host of good were begun at this time.

And as with all revivals, the next generation of ministers came from this one.

HOW LONG?

The length of this revival differed considerably between countries. In Ulster the revival went from autumn 1858 to spring 1860. Wales also started in autumn 1858 until autumn 1860, although meetings went on longer in Cardiff. Scotland began in November 1858 in Aberdeen, but there does not seem to be another outbreak until September 1859 in Glasgow. It mostly ended in the Autumn of 1861, although there are some outliers, like a big revival in the Shetlands in 1863.

England is more difficult to evaluate – as there were a few outbreaks in the autumn of 1859, but it does not seem to have got going until early 1860. As for its end, there seem to be several occurrences all the way through to 1866.

Why these differences? I have thought a lot about this. The smallness of Ulster and Wales both in population and land mass, together with the dominance of some denominations leads me to think that the fire of revival spread more quickly and reached saturation point much faster; this would help explain the relative shortness of their revivals.

I cannot explain the delay in England so easily. Perhaps it was to do with the Church of England not being united behind the revival and also the relatively huge land mass over which the news had to travel. Perhaps it was because many of the main itinerant revivalists were busy in the other countries.

The longevity in England is also interesting. I can only think again that this is because England was huge compared to the other home nations and it took time for the revival fires to get around the country. This would partly have been due to there not being enough evangelists.

NUMBERS

Generally speaking the Presbyterian, Congregationalist, Baptist and Methodist churches were all for the revival, although, the different Methodist denominations did ban itinerant revivalists from their churches because many ministers were jealous and wanted to maintain control of their area.

Anglican evangelicals were supportive, but the liberals were indifferent and the High Church Anglicans and Catholics opposed the revival outright.

Estimating the numbers saved during the revival is difficult. Edwin Orr got hold of most of the available data to estimate that 100,000 were converted in Ulster; about 110,000 in Wales; and 300,000 in Scotland. I think that Ulster and Wales are pretty solid as the Presbyterian church and the Methodists kept good annual records.

A Scottish historian I know and respect is quite critical of the 300,000 in Scotland, but I am more supportive of it. The problem with Scotland is that five out of six people were considered members of a church, so, if they came properly to the Lord during the revival, they would probably not be considered an addition. After reading all the accounts I have, it seems to me that Scotland was considerably impacted with revival fires, as much as Ulster or Wales were, so I do not think it unreasonable to think that similarly 10% of the population was saved. There are also many accounts of church members being saved and one must remember the enormous number of children who were saved, as they probably would not have been counted as church members.

Here are some contemporary comments about the revival in Scotland:

The 1858-64 Revival

"It was said that four-fifths of households of the parish had 'a day of visitation' from the Lord and in most of them one or two have been hopefully converted. The work also spread to adjoining parishes."

"More than half the population of 280 of the Orkney Island of Foula was converted."

"There is scarcely a house where there has not been some awakening, less or more. In one house we can count not less than eight converts."

"At Findochty, I understand that, with but few exceptions, the whole village may be said to have found the Truth."

England is again difficult to estimate. Orr researched as much as he could and came up with 250,000 added to the Church of England, 100,000 to the Baptists, 70,000 to the Congregationalists and 200,000 to the Methodists. This totals 620,000 and probably does not take into account children, 2% pa dying, emigration, existing members being converted or those converted who never joined a church. With a population of nineteen million, this represents 3.75% saved in England which to me does not sound unreasonable.

In total this comes to over 1.1 million and represents the largest ever revival in the United Kingdom. Do it again Lord!

WHAT CAN WE LEARN?

What can we learn from the revival that we can perhaps apply to the one we are waiting for.

We have been waiting a long time for the expected billion

soul revival. I personally have been expecting ten million conversions for the UK; ten times that of the 1858 revival.

Reaching Different Groups

What I read about reaching different groups in London, such as hop pickers, lamplighters and prostitutes, I thought was brilliant.

Demographics have shifted hugely since 1858 with now over 90% of our population living in cities. If we do not learn how to take a city for Christ, a future revival will not be successful. We need an inclusive strategy to reach different people groups.

Like this revival, the strategy I mentioned earlier should include different denominations across ethnic communities, itinerant ministers, and the ministry of all believers.

Helpers

The 1858 revival in England was not as successful as it might have been had there been more helpers. When the revival comes we must be ready to send out anyone and everyone to bring in the lost. Training people now would be a step forward. Happily, we have quite a number of young people who have been to Bethel, International House of Prayer, Toronto, etc., who will be wonderful evangelists in the coming awakening.

Pastoring

From my research it seemed to me that particularly in Ulster and Wales, the revival ended because pastors felt that they needed to look after the converts, so they shut down bringing in more of the harvest.

I think it is very important for pastors to prepare their churches into two parts; one evangelistic and one pastoral, so that both can go on at the same time. While one side is bringing in the lost, the other teaches and equips the converts to help them persevere in their faith.

The pastoral element must include how to teach and equip the converts for their new lives, much like this revival did in seeing success in people continuing as followers of Christ.

Prayer

Clearly prayer is a massive part of revival. We should be asking the Lord now for the gift of travailing prayer and for the spirit of prayer to be poured out. Today, there is definitely not enough of either going on in our nation.

Unity

Vital for any revival as I mentioned earlier. We are not bad at this these days; pastors of different denominations get together to pray quite regularly, which is great. We must encourage every church to be involved, especially the Church of England.

The number of conversions in any general awakening is only limited by the number of workers and the number of ministers open to the work. If any group or church does not want to get involved, then there will be fewer conversions.

Health

Several itinerant revivalists in this revival were taken out for a time due to their health. It will be very important for those of you busy in the coming revival to look after your health.

The 1858-64 Revival

Revival is like an addiction; seeing God move is something you will not want to miss in case God's hand is lifted, but as you have seen with this revival, it went on for over a year; several years in parts, so there will be plenty of time. It will be a marathon not a sprint!

Testimony

This is such an important part of revival. Go to where revival is and bring it back. Encourage new believers to testify as to what happened to them.

Conversions

Everyone seems to be saying that the coming revival is going to be different. Now this may be so, especially as far as technology goes, but in one way I hope we will revert back to the days of the 1858 revival where people were convicted of sin, awakened to Jesus and then rejoiced in their salvation. In this revival the people were not asked to repeat some words by a pastor and that was their conversion experience; a good portion of the converted had an encounter with God.

A minister and an individual summarised well what the revival meant to them:

The minister, "A year ago I was preaching to the dead, but now I am preaching to the living." The individual, "Before the revival, in which I had no faith, my house was like a wee hell; now, it is like a wee heaven!"

One observer wrote:

> "I cannot help speaking of the radiant joy that beams in the countenance - it must be seen to be believed. My own heart has been filled with gladness and happiness in looking upon this

shining forth of the Spirit's witness, and this leads me at once to trace the source of this radiance; it is this - all the believers have the assurance of salvation; not the hope merely, but the precious assured reality. I must note the earnestness of the newly awakened souls for the conversion of others. Both old and young, as soon as they themselves have tasted of the heavenly grace, bring all their heaven-born love and energy to the Saviour's feet, that others may be partakers of the like precious promises. Let us who have long known Christ, go and do likewise."

Amen

This chapter came from many sources, but particularly the "Revival Newspaper."

Chapter Five

1873-75 Moody Awakeing

The 1873-75 Awakening is often referred to as D. L. Moody's Revival, but is that correct? God was already powerfully moving in the south of England in March 1873, and in the north in April, then later on in Nottingham. There was a widespread awakening in the West of Cornwall and the Salvation Army was doing powerful work in London.

Moody was only one amongst others who tapped into what was already happening in the United Kingdom, but history shows that large revivals/awakenings do not begin with an evangelist – they begin with God. He/she recognises the season and then acts as God's messenger and lights the fire. I believe that most pastors do not recognise the 'seasons', but evangelists, by the nature of their work automatically tap into God's plans and purposes whenever He is hovering over the land.

EARLY LIFE

Dwight Lyman Moody was born in 1837 in Northfield, Massachusetts, into a Unitarian family. When he was seventeen, he was fed up with country life and one day made an instant decision that he would go into some business or other in Boston; so he packed his bags and left to make his fortune. One of his uncles offered him a job in his shoe business on the understanding that he would go to church and Sunday school. With great charisma, a natural understanding of business and extraordinary energy he was a very successful salesman.

As per his promise, Moody joined a lively Congregational church and a Sunday school. After a while, his teacher thought the time was right for Moody to accept Jesus as his Saviour, so he went to visit him at the shoe shop. He simply told Moody how much Christ loved him and what He expected in return and that was it - Moody was born again.

In 1856, now nineteen, Moody moved to the new and exciting city of Chicago, where he immediately got involved in the Jeremiah Lamphier Revival that was sweeping across America. This was his first, the first of many.

He got employment at a shoe company and he applied to lead a class at a small mission school. However, at the time they had more teachers than they required, so he was told that he would be welcome if he provided his own class. On the following Sunday, he arrived at the school leading a procession of eighteen little 'hoodlums' that he had gathered. It was a sign of things to come.

In 1858, at the age of twenty-one, Moody set out to start a mission school on a larger scale in another part of the city. He was very successful, and the work later developed into the Illinois Street Church. The Sunday school grew to six hundred people which included parents of the children. Clearly, Moody had a really magnetic personality, but he was not yet an evangelist.

By 1860 Moody realised his Christian work on the surface was prospering as he could gather up to fifteen hundred people on a Sunday, but he realised that none of them were actually converted. Then one day something happened that changed everything.

There was a class of young girls in the school who were very badly behaved, and their teacher came to Moody to tell him that he had had a haemorrhage in his lungs and the doctor said that he would soon die. He explained that he was extremely troubled because he had to leave Chicago, but he had never led any of his class to Christ. Moody suggested that he went to visit each one of the class and tell them how he felt and he agreed to go with him from house to house. The teacher spoke to the first young lady about the state of her soul and she soon had tears welling up. But they both prayed and the girl gave her life to Christ. They went to other houses and it was not long before each one broke down and sought salvation. At the end of ten days, the teacher came to Moody's store and with a shining face, told him that the last of his class had given her life to Christ.

Moody wrote:

> "He had to leave the next night, so I called his class together that night for a prayer meeting and there God kindled a fire in my soul that has never gone out. The height of my ambition had been to be a successful merchant and if I had known that meeting was going to take that ambition out of me, I might not have gone. But how many times I have thanked God since for that meeting! The dying teacher sat in the midst of his class and talked with them and read the 14th chapter of John. We knelt to pray and I was just rising from my knees when one of the class began to pray for her dying teacher. Another prayed and another, before we rose the whole class had prayed."

The next evening he went to the train station to say goodbye to the teacher and without prearrangement each one of the class came to say goodbye. The last they saw of the teacher was his finger pointing upward, telling the class to meet him in heaven.

1873-75 Moody Awakening

So, Moody put aside his desire to make a fortune and instead go into full-time ministry. The next year the American Civil War broke out. Moody did not join up because he could never kill anybody. He had been a member of the Young Men's Christian Association (YMCA) since 1854 and was a huge supporter all his life. With two others, he formed a branch of this organisation to hold services for soldiers who passed through Chicago; after a while the Union soldiers left to go and fight and Confederate prisoners took their place. One day Moody and a friend went in to hold a service and the Presence of God fell, impacting dozens of the prisoners – many were converted over the next two or three weeks.

Moody visited the front lines many times during the Civil War. The work of his committee was to; arrange for the preaching of the gospel, distribute free Bibles, and visit the sick and wounded in hospitals. They ministered to Union and Confederate soldiers alike. Meetings were held everywhere and many a camp became the scene of a deep and effective revival.

At the close of the war in 1865 Moody returned to Chicago and Sunday School work. His mission school in Chicago was a revelation. People came from all around to see how it worked and copied it. He used novel methods to fill his schools, using oranges and sweets and other things to draw them in. He looked after them, visiting their homes if they did not appear at the school and he took such a warm and practical interest in them that they became devotedly attached to him.

Moody began holding conferences to tell people about his methods and experiences in his Sunday school work. Thousands would come and the State of Illinois put its weight behind his work.

It was then that Moody started a daily prayer meeting at

noon which became a very important part of his ministry and of the Awakening in the UK.

Moody was an evangelist through and through. He would stand in the streets inviting passers-by to come to the noonday prayer meeting. During the summer months, he would be seen outside every night preaching in the streets. He would also visit prisoners and the sick.

In 1867, Moody came to England to learn from the great orators, such as Spurgeon. In London he went to the YMCA in Aldersgate Street where he established a noon prayer meeting. This grew very quickly and started to spread across England. People were very interested in his gospel preaching methods and in the three months he was there he became quite popular.

In 1870, Moody met Ira Sankey, a gospel singer. On being introduced he told him he was just the person that he had been looking for to help him in his work in Chicago. Sankey was not sure but the next day he went to help Moody with an open-air service. Sankey wrote:

> "The address that evening was one as powerful I had ever heard. The crowd stood spellbound at the burning words and many a tear was brushed away from the eyes of the men as they looked up into the speaker's honest face."

Some months later Sankey agreed to join Moody.

The next year Moody did a series of talks on major characters in the Bible which attracted the largest congregation he had spoken to. After ten Sundays, five of which he spoke on Jesus, he asked them to go home and think about their souls before coming back for the last Sunday in the series. However, that week there was the Great Chicago Fire and his congregation never came together again. It was because of this that Moody decided that whenever he preached, he must make people decide for Christ then and there.

That same year, Moody noticed two women praying for him during each service. He asked them why and was told they were praying for him for power. This puzzled Moody as he felt he already had power with many being saved under his ministry, so he asked them to come and see him to explain further. They told him that they wanted him to receive the filling of the Holy Spirit and as they said that he felt a great hunger come into him. He became desperate to be filled with Holy Spirit, although he was not sure what that meant.

He started calling out to God to be filled with Holy Spirit, until one day when he was in New York, "I can only say that God revealed Himself to me and I had such an experience of His love that I had to ask Him to stay His hand." His preaching did not seem to change but hundreds were converted. He had been baptised with the Holy Spirit and Fire.

In June 1872, Moody decided to return to England for a short trip. He came to study but was nudged by Holy Spirit to change his plans and accepted an invitation to speak in a North London church.

There was a bed-ridden member of the church there who had heard about Moody and she had been praying for months for God to send him to her church!

The morning service seemed very dead but at the 6:30 pm service it seemed that the very atmosphere was charged with the Spirit of God. When he finished preaching, he asked that anybody who wanted to become a Christian should stand up and people rose all over the church until it seemed that everyone was standing on their feet. He directed them to the inquiry room, (something that was central to the coming awakening) which they packed into. Both he and the minister were amazed.

This clearly proves that prayer is a vital ingredient of any awakening.

The next day Moody went to Dublin, but on the Tuesday morning he received a note urging him to return to London as the pastor wrote that there were more inquirers on Monday than on Sunday. So, Moody returned and held meetings for ten days and four hundred were saved in those meetings.

On his return to America, Moody, who had made a very good impression while in England, received three invitations to return to do evangelistic work, with a promise that funds would be available to meet his expenses and those of his party. He decided to accept them and make another short visit to England. He wanted a gospel singer to accompany him, but his first two choices were unavailable, so he took Ira Sankey. Unexpectedly, the funds for their passage did not arrive, so Moody had to use all his savings to buy the tickets. Just as well he did because this trip changed his life.

UK MISSION

Moody and Sankey reached Liverpool on June 17th, 1873 where a letter was waiting for him to tell him that all three of the leaders who had invited him had died, which explained why no funds had arrived. On arriving at their hotel Moody found an unopened letter that he had received before sailing from New York. It was from the secretary, George Bennett of the YMCA in York. The letter invited him to speak at the Association. Moody replied to say that he was coming to York to begin some meetings. Bennett replied, "give me a month", to which Moody replied, "we are coming tomorrow!" On arriving in York, they asked for local pastors to provide a pulpit for that Sunday and two Wesleyan, a Baptist and a Congregational Church were put at his disposal.

The first ten days of meetings in York were not really successful, however, the movement broke surface on the second Wednesday in the Wesleyan chapel. Someone wrote, "the Holy Spirit's powers mightily manifested and anxious souls were all over the building. The aged Chapel Superintendent seemed paralysed by astonishment and could do nothing but weep for joy."

The following day they went to the new Baptist Church. The minister was a young man who really did not think that Moody did anything different to what he did, but he had extended an invitation to the Americans anyway.

Many years later he wrote:

> "I was a young pastor then and bound rather rigidly by the chains of conventionalism. Such had been my training, and such might have been my career. But here was a revelation of a new ideal. The little vestry there - how vividly I remember it! - was the scene of our long and earnest prayers as we knelt around the leather-covered table in the middle of the room. I remember that Mr Moody, at the great Free Trade Hall, Manchester, referred to that little room as the fountain from which the river of blessing for the whole country had sprung."

The glory of God descended into this church, which was crowded each service and many gave their lives to Jesus. The woman who taught the senior girls' class in the church, had been so gripped by Moody relating the story of the dying Sunday School teacher that she missed her midday lunch to pray. At teachers' tea the minister asked casually,

"Well, Miss Lines, how have you got on this afternoon?"
"Oh, I told that story again and I believe every one of my girls has given her heart to God!"

The young Baptist minister was amazed at this. He watched people giving their lives to Christ in his parlour and learned about conversion for the first time. The pastor's name was F B Meyer, who went on to write seventy books, selling five million copies and became one of the most influential ministers of his day. Years later he said he owed everything to the time he had in his parlour, watching people's conversions.

There is an important lesson here. What would have happened had Meyer been offended by the different way Moody did things and not invited him to his church. He would probably have missed his destiny!

Next Moody and Sankey went to Sunderland where the meetings were disappointing. The minister who invited him put it down to lack of unity, with only two or three ministers co-operating and he inferred that one of the ministers was working actively against the mission.

Newcastle was where the meetings got packed out from the start and there were many salvations. Their itinerary then took them from Newcastle to Darlington, Bishop Auckland, Stockton and Carlisle, before heading to Scotland at the end of 1873.

But it had looked like the overall campaign might fizzle out when a minister from Leith, near Edinburgh came to one of the meetings and then invited them to Edinburgh, with the promise that there would be a committee of Free and established church ministers to organise and prepare for the visit.

Edinburgh was where they made a name for themselves.

1873-75 Moody Awakening

The dour Calvinists of Scotland were surprised by Holy Spirit and the love and forgiveness of the Father.

They were nine months in Scotland where they ministered in twenty-five cities and towns. Then three months in Northern Ireland, mostly in Belfast, but also Londonderry. Followed by Manchester, Sheffield, Birmingham, Liverpool and finally four months in London.

Over the two years Moody and Sankey were in the United Kingdom, the results of their labours were much the same everywhere they went.

PREPARATION

It is very important to understand that this was not Moody's Awakening, it was Holy Spirit's. Holy Spirit was on the move in different parts of the country before Moody arrived. He was preparing the way and hovering over the nation. Moody and Sankey were the main men chosen to light the fire in many towns and cities. The country was full of expectation and needed a fire ignitor. I believe that there was one big Awakening from 1858-1884, as there was the 185-64 Awakening, then this one in 1873-5 and then the huge expansion of the Salvation Army in 1877-84 (see the next chapter).

Humanly speaking these were probably the best prepared meetings ever. Once Moody realised the importance of unity, he made sure that there were committees of ministers from all denominations set up to prepare for his visits. That, together with the unified prayer meetings that sometimes went on for months before a visit, played a huge part in their success. It was definitely an advantage that many of the visits were planned months in advance.

A unique advertising strategy applied in some cities was designed by Reginald Radcliffe, who was one of the main leaders of the 1858-64 awakening. He divided big cities like Manchester, Liverpool and London into small districts and arranged for helpers to visit every single home to deliver a leaflet about the meetings and to speak to people about the gospel.

Another aspect of the mission was the enormous popularity of Sankey's hymns. These went ahead of them wherever they went and helped promote the mission. Most awakenings have their own music.

Newspapers also played a role, in that their mostly kind reports, advertised the meetings to the public.

Someone wrote, "The windows of every bookseller are hung with their pictures. Penny editions of Mr Sankey's songs are hawked about the streets."

Even the railway stations had placards to catch the travellers for their meetings. The papers reported their services with a fulness never dreamed of before in reporting religious meetings.

MOODY AND SANKEY

It was said that Moody preached the gospel and Sankey sang the gospel. Sankey was thought by some to be as important as Moody in evangelising the mass of people. His songs were mainly to do with telling the gospel story rather than praising God.

An observer wrote this about Moody's preaching:

> "Mr Moody's preaching is intensely earnest; he speaks because he believes the vital importance of the truth he utters, and not simply because he is expected to say something. His power of illustration is marvellous, both for its freshness and its pathos.

> Sometimes the effect of some illustration, nearly always taken from his own life and experience, is so great, that the most hardened feel their hearts smitten and drawn into sympathy with the truth and are drawn towards Jesus as their Saviour and their Friend. Words utterly fail to convey an adequate idea of the power of the simple and thrilling presentation of the truth at these gospel services; and the power can only be accounted for on the ground that the Spirit of God, without noise and excitement, but in the calm, clear utterances of divine truth, attests to the power of the Word to awaken, convince, and convert the hearts of men."

Sadly, some were put off by his American accent, his vulgarity, (which I think is referring to his lack of religious pomposity), his fast speaking and of course the fact that he was not ordained. There are always leaders who are put off by personal attributes whilst ignoring the substance of the message.

Of Sankey, a minister wrote:

> "Mr Sankey sings appropriate sacred solos, the congregation often taking up the 'refrain' - a novelty which to hear is startling to the traditionalists of religion, but which to hear, at once commanded solemnity, acquiescence, and gratification. Nothing can be further from 'performance' than his performance. The man and the music disappear in the sentiment. The sound enforces the sense but does not supersede it - every word and every syllable are distinctly uttered and distinctly heard. He sings the gospel with persuasive effect, throwing his whole soul, not into the accompaniment, but into the song, the sentiment of which lights up his face, not with the glitter of art, but with the glory of unfeigned sympathy."

Due to the popularity of the songs there was an increasing demand for a book of them to be published. Unfortunately, English publishers were not keen based upon a similar book not being successful. Moody was therefore forced to offer a guarantee against losses to have the hymn book published. The book was published and within two months there were two more print runs.

Moody was keen that nobody should accuse him or Sankey of greed (this did not stop that from happening), so they both agreed to give up all rights to royalties. By the time they got to London £5,000 had accrued in royalties, but Moody insisted that the money be given away. By 1885 the royalties amounted to a staggering $357,388 (around £9 million today) all of which was given to charities.

Moody did not receive any remuneration during the two years he was in the UK. He only accepted enough to pay expenses and those of their families, which had been the original agreement before they arrived in the country.

One day, on the train from Glasgow to Edinburgh, Sankey read an anonymous poem that he thought might be made into a hymn. At the meeting in Edinburgh, Moody asked him to play a hymn with a solo, that was suitable for ending the meeting, the theme of which was the 'Good Shepherd.' Sankey did not have one, but he kept hearing a voice telling him to play the hymn he found on the train. He finally gave in, trusting the Lord to give him the tune. He played a first verse and then repeated the tune, note for note with subsequent verses. The hymn made a deep impact on everyone, bringing many to tears. 'The Ninety and Nine.' became his most popular hymn,.

THE MEETINGS

Moody created a model for the week's meetings and he used it everywhere. There were normally some weeks/

months of united prayer meetings to prepare before their visit. The longer the time that the prayer meetings went on for, the quicker the impact once the meetings had started.

Moody would always begin with a meeting for Christian workers, where sometimes several thousand attended. The purpose was to encourage them to step out in their calling and to get them to help in the mission, mainly praying or evangelising. Holy Spirit was always powerfully in these meetings, so many got enthusiastic and took part in the mission.

Every weekday there was the noon prayer meeting which was considered a vital part of the mission. Sometimes a few thousand would attend each day. For the people of those times, it was very informal. It would start with a hymn, followed by prayers for people who had written in asking for prayer. This went on for about fifteen minutes and God answered many of these prayers during this awakening. Then there would be another hymn, a short talk from the leader and then thirty minutes for people to give short testimonies, pray etc:

> "The noon prayer meetings present a more wonderful sight than ever. To say they are crowded does not express half the interest. One must be a witness and a daily witness for himself to fully understand the spirit of prayer and trust and hope, and gladness that pervades the people who come together."

In the afternoons there were bible studies which were to have a lasting impact on the people, who went away with a hunger to read the bible. There were also inquiry meetings after the afternoon Bible studies allowing people opportunity to give their lives to Jesus.

In the evenings there was a full evangelistic service. It would be during this meeting when people would be impressed by Holy Spirit and would be awakened to the reality of their sin. These would always be packed, with one or two other buildings acting as overflows - clearly health and safety today would not allow so many in a building!

The meetings had ministers from most denominations on the platform either side of Moody and the meeting began with about half an hour of hymns:

> "The music and singing (he would sing the solo, but quickly teach the congregation the chorus) not only drew sinners to hear but was eminently used of God to break down and melt their hearts. Sankey played with matchless feeling and touching tenderness, and a heart full of love for souls. Many were won for Christ during the tour through the gospel truths that were sung."

After the singing, there would be prayer for those who had sent in prayer requests. In his sermon Moody usually dealt with a theme rather than a text, illustrating the point by giving examples from all through the bible. After the sermon Sankey sang a hymn and Moody prayed for the unconverted; then he would call for an inquiry meeting for those who wanted to know Jesus. This was the result of the Chicago fire - he wanted people to make a decision for Christ there and then and not wait for the enemy to try to dissuade them in the coming days. Those who indicated they wanted Jesus were taken to another room where Moody and Christian workers would point them to Christ. The majority who were saved on this tour gave their lives to Jesus at this meeting.

This would often be followed by a meeting for young men. Moody considered young men to be his main target as they would be the leaders of the future. This too was followed by an inquiry meeting.

Occasionally, Moody chaired a meeting to discuss subjects such as, how to reach the masses, how to run prayer meetings, how to conduct inquiry meetings, how to secure the young for Christ and to highlight what difficulties were presenting themselves. Awakenings do not just happen; they need a lot of planning and organising.

Normally after the first week of meetings in a town, Moody would set up a weekly meeting for the new converts. The idea was to give the new converts a good foundation. They would explain what they had been trying to do for Christ and would discuss any doubts or misunderstandings the converts had. One minister wrote:

> "No one can come to see these young converts and hear them speaking out of the fulness of their hearts to the praise and glory of Him who has called them out of darkness into His marvellous light, without feeling this work is truly of God."

Moody recognised that in Scotland there was a reticence among the leaders to use young converts. He said, "The spirit of the gospel is get and give... I believe that if hundreds of young converts were setting to work they would do immense good." A dozen years earlier the testimony of new converts was a powerful weapon in that big revival, so it is strange that the ministers had not learned from that.

Also, special services were put on for specific groups of people, women, men, children, teachers, shipbuilders, warehouse girls, etc. Working men seldom came to the big meetings, so meetings were put on especially for them and these were usually held away from church buildings; like in theatres or Assembly Rooms.

Trains and other modes of transport would be overflowing, and hordes of people could be seen walking along the streets to the meetings. In Liverpool and London a building was erected purely for the length of Moody's mission, holding 10,000+ and the Agricultural Hall in London held over 17,000. In London buildings were hired/or built in the north, south, east and west of the city. Apart from some cities like London, Birmingham and Liverpool, most meetings were held in the biggest churches in the town.

Buildings were filled within minutes of opening. This, as usual in an awakening, caused problems because Christians just wanted to hear more and more, so the unsaved had a problem finding a seat. From some accounts the Church was in a fairly moribund state, so Christians needed to be in the meetings to be fired up, but then they need to move out to serve the Lord and allow the unsaved in. This is an important point to note for the coming revival.

To cater for this the organisers had to make some meetings 'tickets only' to ensure that the right type of person came to the meeting. Moody recognised this, noting that it was a problem that was greater in London than elsewhere:

> "It's time for Christians to stop coming here and crowding into the best seats. It's time for them to go out among these sailors and drunkards and bring them in and give them the best seats."

Once Moody and Sankey had established a work in a city; other evangelists would come and help multiply the fruit. In Newcastle for instance, Henry Moorehouse came, so instead of one meeting there were two each evening and sometimes there were three when a local minister might join in. Moody knew he needed help with the young men, so he asked Henry Drummond to follow him from town to town and lead the young men's meetings. Moody called him the most Christ-like man he had ever met.

The final meeting in Glasgow was held in the Botanical Gardens on the following Sunday:

> "Mr Sankey found his way into the building and began the service with six or seven thousand, who were crushed together there; but so great was the crowd outside, estimated at twenty to thirty thousand people, that Mr Moody himself could not get inside. Standing on the coachman's box of the carriage in which he was driven, he asked the members of the choir to sing. They found a place for themselves on the roof of a low shed near the building, and after they had sung Mr Moody preached for an hour on 'Immediate Salvation.' So distinct was his voice that the great crowd could hear him without difficulty. The evening was beautiful, the air calm, the sun near its setting; the deep green foliage of the trees that enclosed the grounds framed the scene."

Writing of this, a witness said:

> "After the sermon, Mr Moody asked all those who wished to attend the inquiry meeting to enter the Palace. Those who could remain were requested to gather in the neighbouring church, Kelvinside, for prayer. In a few minutes the Crystal Palace was filled, and when Mr Moody asked for those who were unsaved and yet anxious to be saved, two thousand people rose to their feet."

UNITY AND OPPOSITION

One of the most visible fruits of the awakening was unity. Unity was a major reason for the success of the mission.

Sunderland was not successful because only two or three ministers got involved. There was no unity there and as a result, little fruit. There were also unity problems elsewhere.

Scotland had not recovered from the big denominational split of the 'Disruption' in 1843. There was competition and mistrust amongst Scottish ministers. A pastor in the Highlands, Dr Kennedy of Dingwall, wrote a paper called "Hyper Evangelism 'Another Gospel' Though a Mighty Power." Kennedy was a very respected minister from the Highlands, who had been involved in revivals in the past. Kennedy was clearly not happy with the revival at all. Dr Kennedy, now getting on in years, believed in a form of Calvinism that did not allow any divergence. One of his main disagreements was with the idea that you could become a Christian there and then; in the Highlands they normally required proof of several months of good Christian living before deciding if they were saved or not.

In the south of Scotland there was another very respected minister called Horatius Bonar, who wrote a paper opposing that written by Kennedy. Both these ministers were part of the Free Church of Scotland which had broken away from the Church of Scotland in 1843. They were supposedly on the same side, but in this they were diametrically opposed to one another. However, Bonar, although disagreeing with some aspects of Moody's ministry, realised that in the important areas he could agree with Moody, whilst disagreeing with some of the less important ones. Basically, Kennedy threw the baby out with the bath water, whereas Bonar did not. Fortunately, this disagreement did not seem to impact the move of God in Scotland to any important degree.

Two weeks into the Scottish mission thirty-eight of the leading ministers and laymen of Edinburgh sent a circular to all the ministers in Scotland, pointing out the good work that was going on and asking for united prayer that the movement would go all over Scotland. The letter described what was the most remarkable feature of the meetings:

"...It is the presence and the power of the Holy Spirit, the solemn awe, the prayerful, believing, expectant spirit, the anxious inquiry of united souls, and the longing of believers to grow more like Christ - their hungering and thirsting after holiness."

The sectarian divisions which were so visible in ecclesiastical and social life, melted away when people got together to serve God in this awakening.

Northern Ireland of course had its sectarianism, but the unity between Presbyterians, Episcopalians and Baptists was excellent, even if the Catholics were mostly absent from the mission.

England had its own problems. The unity between the non-conformist churches was excellent; the Anglicans were the problem. Moody recognised this problem early on, refusing to go to London until there was more evidence of unity. In order to help with this, he asked a wealthy London businessman to organise a fund of £2,000 (£280,000 today) to pay for the "Christian" newspaper (formerly "The Revival"), which had been so successful in the 1858-64 awakening in stirring up people through all the testimonies in it, to be sent to every minister in the UK for thirteen weeks.

When the Moody and Sankey arrived in Manchester the city had been holding united evangelistic services for eight months in nearly all the non-conformist churches in the district. The Anglicans were not involved it seems, so Moody sent out a letter to all the Anglican clergy in the city, begging them to join in as unity was so important to the results of the meetings. Anglicans should have been right behind the movement and the vicars should have encouraged their congregations to go to the meetings and

1873-75 Moody Awakening

get involved - some did, but the Archbishop of Canterbury did not endorse the movement, so many stayed away. Archbishop Tait wrote a letter that was published, basically saying he liked Moody and Sankey, was grateful for the work they were doing evangelising the masses, but he could not agree with all that they did, so he could not endorse the mission.

A typically political letter, trying to ingratiate himself with the High Church people who generally opposed the revival and the evangelicals. The lack of direction from the bishops must have damaged the potential fruit from the mission, particularly in London. However, the Anglicans were well involved in Liverpool and the vicar of Sheffield was leading the meetings in his city.

There were some ministers, as ever, who did not take part because the awakening was not manifesting according to what they thought it should look like. Why do so many ignore the fruit in such cases? Most ministers were overjoyed that this awakening was without any noise, I guess many would have rejected it had Holy Spirit manifested loudly.

Rumours circulated to discredit the Americans. They were accused of only doing the tour to make money and that Moody was getting a commission on bibles sold and Sankey was getting a commission on organs. Before big campaigns they would hold a meeting of ministers where they could ask any questions they wanted, including about any rumour they had heard. This was an excellent way to remove any doubts people had.

In Scotland and Northern Ireland, the newspapers were quite respectful towards the pair, but there was some mocking and criticism from the English press, probably initiated by the High Church faction, but things could have been much worse.

You may have noticed that I have not mentioned Wales. This is because Moody only did two last minute meetings in Wrexham, just before he left for America. Sankey was not with him and one of the meetings was very unsuccessful. The Welsh in Liverpool seem to have been very impacted, but I have looked at twenty-two Welsh newspapers over three years and have found less than ten reports of stirrings in Wales and all of them in the North. This rather mystifies me considering the great number of awakenings there had been in Wales over the previous 150 years.

THE FRUIT

Sadly, Moody was not at all interested in numbers, so we have no idea of how many people were saved during the two years of their mission.

More people heard the Gospel preached in this mission than any mission there has ever been in the United Kingdom. It was reported that 2,530,000 were at the meetings in London alone, although of course many came more than once.

Religiosity was broken up:

> "Moody's mission is to break up formalism and show the necessity and power of spirituality. The tendency of human nature the world over is to drop down into forms and allow the spiritual flame to burn very low. In Christian nations that are full of strong defenders of the faith, there have come over many of the churches a stiffness and dullness in prayer meetings and other services that it was necessary to break up."

Does that sound familiar?

A pastor from Manchester wrote:

> "No class received more blessing than the ministers: sermons have changed from formalism into freedom, and from frost into fervour. Prayer meetings, formerly dull as ditch water have been quickened and made alive with more interest and power. Long prayers have been shortened; special services are becoming common; evangelistic effort is on every hand."

As already mentioned, Bible studies, noon prayer meetings, Sankey's hymns, the inquiry meeting and people making decisions for Christ there and then, were all continued after Moody left. For many ministers it was like they had been taught evangelism again.

As is usual in an awakening I have seen reports of police with nothing to do, pubs and theatres losing business, etc.

As for other benefits, someone wrote:

> "A spirit of evangelism was awakened that has never died away. A large number of city missions and other active organisations were established. Denominational differences were buried to a remarkable extent. The clergymen of all denominations were drawn into cooperation on a common platform - the salvation of the lost. Bibles were re-opened, and Bible study received a wonderful impetus. Long-standing prejudices were swept away. New life was infused into all methods of Christian activity. An impetus was given to the cause of Temperance such as had not been experienced in Great Britain before."

SPREADING BEYOND MOODY AND SANKEY

Moody and Sankey lit some fires, but Holy Spirit was all over the United Kingdom, waiting for anyone to recognise the season they were in. In many places they were the catalyst, but then others took over the baton.

They went to Berwick-on-Tweed for just one day, but they lit a fire that went on for two years. Ministers of all denominations came from surrounding towns and villages and it spread around the district.

In big cities like Edinburgh and Glasgow, Moody preached and had great results and he inspired other ministers there to go and do likewise. Edinburgh became the religious centre of the country in a way it had not been since the days of John Knox. Towns and villages caught fire around it. A senior minister in Scotland said that you could hardly preach the gospel in Glasgow without great results.

Two months after Moody and Sankey left, there were reports of Holy Spirit moving powerfully in Belfast and particularly in County Antrim and County Down. Evangelistic services were going on in every district of the city.

One minister wrote:

> "Manchester, I am pleased to say, is now on fire. The most difficult of all English cities, perhaps to be set on fire by anything but politics, it is now fairly ablaze and the flames are breaking out in all directions."

Also, the news of what was happening in the cities would reach the surrounding neighbourhoods and requests would come in for people to visit there. Different countries created an Evangelism Society and then, using existing and newly saved evangelists, sent them out two by two to answer the call and to light the fires in churches all over the country. We could do well to organise such societies today to be ready for when the Awakening comes.

Other pastors heard what was happening and took it on themselves to start something in their area. A pastor in Bolton organised a pastors' conference, started a noon prayer meeting, exchanged pulpits with pastors of other denominations and organised special services!

There were areas all over the nation, from the Shetlands to West Cornwall where fires were lit where there was no connection at all to Moody, because Holy Spirit was hovering over the nation.

LEAVING

Moody and Sankey left the United Kingdom in August 1875. They had worked tirelessly over the two years they were here and appear to have had very little time off. Drummond noted Moody's schedule in London:

> "A three-mile drive to noon meeting; lunch; Bible-reading at 3.30 pm, followed by inquiry meeting till at least five; then a five-mile drive to East End to preach to twelve thousand at 8.30 pm; then inquiry meeting; five or six-mile drive home. This is every day this week and next - a terrible strain, which, however, he never seems to feel for a moment."

Lord Shaftesbury thanked God publicly that Mr Moody had not been educated at Oxford:

> "for he had a wonderful power of getting at the hearts of men, and while the common people hear him gladly, many persons of high station have been greatly struck with the marvellous simplicity and power of his preaching."

Lord Shaftesbury added that the Lord Chancellor a short time before had said to him:

> "The simplicity of that man's preaching, the clear manner in which he sets forth salvation by Christ, is to me the most striking and the most delightful thing I ever knew in my life."

CONCLUSION

It had been an extraordinary time, with many salvations, but how impactful was it on society going forward? I am afraid I have no idea, because, as with all awakenings, no historian ever thinks of going back to answer this question.

I read an 1878 article that points out that there had been many conferences to try to work out "How to reach the masses," but the writer said that there had been very little fruit from them. 'The Christian' at one time in 1878 had weekly reports from some evangelists belonging to the Evangelistic Association. At one point they wrote that there were 130 meetings held by their evangelists on a Sunday with around 40,000 hearers.

1878 also was the start of the huge expansion of the Salvation Army which came about because William Booth found a way to reach the masses. There was a greater desire by ministers to call for the help of evangelists and for individuals to evangelise their friends and neighbours, I have seen several comments from ministers saying that things will change, but nothing to show that it did.

A Liverpool minister wrote, "We can never be as we have been" and let us hope that that will be the reality for the next Awakening.

This chapter came from many sources but mainly Christian Newspapers of the time.

Chapter Six

The Rise of the Salvation Army

At first glance one might wonder why I have included the history of the Salvation Army in a book on revivals. My contention is that the extraordinary growth of the Salvation Army could only have occurred during an Awakening. It is my belief that there was one Awakening from 1858, all the way to 1883.

Early days

William and Catherine Booth were both born in 1829. William was born to a well-off father, but sadly his dad went on to lose it all. After his death, William's mother had to move to very lowly accommodations and William grew up observing great poverty and misery around him. This was something he never forgot and became the foundation for the important ministry that was ahead of him. His salvation experience, together with receiving the Baptism of Fire in a James Caughey (American evangelist) meeting when he was seventeen, set a fire in him to see souls saved. The passion for reformation and for seeing people come to Jesus, combined in William to make him the extraordinary man he was to become.

Some years later another major influence was to come into his life - Catherine Mumford, as she was then. Catherine's mother was a strong Christian and was a huge influence, both with regard to her daughter's spirituality and the sharpness of her mind. Catherine wrote, "I cannot remember the time when I had not intense yearnings after God."

Catherine loved to read and she read the Bible cover to cover eight times by the age of twelve. Her health was fragile all her life and, in her childhood, she spent a lot of time resting, which gave her the opportunity to read extensively. She read a great deal about Church history and theology – great preparation for what lay ahead.

At twelve she got involved in the Temperance movement and her compassion for the marginalised became obvious. Catherine loved going to church and hearing sermons.

On William's 23rd birthday they met at a conference and he took Catherine home. During the journey they fell in love and after a lot of discussion and prayer, they were engaged about a month later. Both were passionate and gifted organisers. William was a great leader and Catherine was both clever and knowledgeable; it shows where they overlapped and complimented each other. William was a force of nature; he had an amazing presence about him. Particularly in the early years, Catherine was more the decision-maker. William was usually unsure of what his next step should be, whereas Catherine was always confident in guiding him.

William and Catherine were married in June 1855 and were in love until the day Catherine died.

Catherine helped William in his decision to accept a position from the Methodist Reform Church to be head of their Spalding, Lincolnshire circuit, where he saw a number of salvations. He then moved to the New Connexion Methodists in 1854, where he quickly gained a reputation as an evangelist.

William's evangelistic activities were very successful, but this created jealousy amongst the ministers of the New Connexion, to such an extent that at the 1857 conference a majority banned him from further revivalist activity, and he was appointed to the Brighouse Circuit. This deeply upset them both and they discussed leaving the New Connexion, but William believed in obeying leadership.

He hoped to be released to evangelise at the next conference, but again he was denied and was appointed to Gateshead, with the verbal understanding that he would be released at the next conference. They were at Gateshead for three years. William was very successful there, growing the church hugely. The tragedy was that this period was in the middle of the greatest revival the United Kingdom has ever had and our greatest revivalist was mainly pastoring.

But it is also a time when Catherine stepped into her destiny. On the prompting of the Holy Spirit, she spent two evenings a week visiting the poor in their homes; getting some to give up drink and others to give their lives to Jesus. She soon realised that she was gifted in this area. Shortly afterwards she felt the strong nudging of the Holy Spirit again, so she got up in church and said a few words, which were received with enthusiasm by the congregation. William, who had been saying for some time that she should preach, told her that she would be preaching in the church that evening. Catherine's talk was a great success and from then on invitations flooded in and her life was changed forever.

In January 1861 William had travelled to London to attend a meeting set up by Reginald Radcliffe for 'representatives and friends of all the agencies carrying on the Lord's work in the East End,' out of which came the East London Special Services Committee. William was interested in what was discussed regarding reaching the masses but wrote to Catherine that he could not think of doing anything like that for the moment.

At the 1861 conference the question was raised again about William becoming a full-time revivalist. There were a lot of discussions and it looked as if he was going to be released when at the last moment someone suggested William be appointed to a circuit but on occasion be released for evangelistic work. William knew this would not work because he knew that the circuit he was being appointed to would require all his efforts, but the compromise was voted on and passed. On hearing the result of the vote, Catherine, who was in the gallery, shouted 'Never!' and shortly afterwards they left New Connexion.

After the conference, he came to London again to see if he should be involved in Home Mission work. He visited several well-known evangelists but went away undecided; deciding to watch and pray and wait for the Lord to make things clear.

After leaving the New Connexion Methodists, William and Catherine were asked to do some revival meetings in Cornwall. These resulted in a big revival and the campaign lasted eighteen months. Incredibly, the Methodist denominations banned revivalist meetings in their churches, largely out of jealousy and the fear that the ministers might lose some of their congregations to the Booths. The crazy thing about this was that they were banning the very thing that each of the Methodist denominations were founded on – revivalism. In the middle of the largest revival the UK has known, these major denominations, in effect, put handcuffs on it.

The Methodist churches were the largest churches around, so William had to start thinking about alternative venues. The ironic thing is, had the Methodists not forced William out and had several denominations not banned revivalism, the Salvation Army might never have been born!

During this time Catherine took many meetings herself. After Cornwall there were other missions around the country, all of which were successful. Because large churches were closed to them, they hired secular buildings, such as a

Circus in Cardiff and they had open-air meetings. This was a very depressing time for William who could not work to the fullness of his capabilities. In 1864 they agreed to do separate missions, thereby spreading their influence.

East London

Catherine held extensive meetings in Rotherhithe, London, which opened up the possibilities of other opportunities for her in the area. They had been thinking about a mission in London, so in 1865 they decided to move from Leeds to London, hoping that the Metropolis would open up to William, the way it looked like it was opening for Catherine.

It is probably difficult today to understand the condition of those living in the slums of the East End of London in the 1860's. Most of the people lived in total squalor with little food and some died of starvation. Sanitation was terrible, as was the sickness, over-crowding and destitution. Their situation was particularly bad in the mid-1860s because the American Civil War had disrupted trade. The extreme poverty that most of the inhabitants were living in got even worse for many.

Another major ingredient to the condition of people living here was drink. In 1830 Parliament was so concerned about the amount of spirits that were being consumed that they passed a bill that allowed cheap licences for the selling of beer and cider. As a result, by 1869 there were over 49,000 licensed beer shops. Someone wrote that in Whitechapel Road one could see nearly 19,000 people go into public houses on a Sunday. Of course, the spending of wages on drink exacerbated the financial stress on most families. Small wonder that the Temperance Movement was very active at this time.

Many had tried to reach Londoners ever since the 1858-64 revival began. That revival was the first time nondenominational evangelists were used to reach the lost. Dozens of them tried hard to evangelise the poorer areas of London, but with only marginal success. It was also the time when new organisations were started to reach the destitute.

The Booths came to the idea that the best way to reach the masses was by an organisation that was independent of the Church. They were also drawn towards London as it was a big enough mission field for them both and so would not require much separation. William however hesitated as he thought that he was not up to the enormous task. He decided to try it, recognising that if he failed, he could still minister in the provinces. It was agreed that he would join Catherine after she had completed a series of meetings in Rotherhithe, and they would decide where to go from there. Her meetings were successful, and the Booths took a house in Shaftesbury Road, Hammersmith, from where they could start their London mission.

In June 1865 William was walking down Whitechapel Road, opposite the Blind Beggar pub when he came across a group of Gospel missioners, who were just finishing a meeting. Some of the people were from The Christian Community (originally formed by the Huguenots in the 17th century) and others were connected to the East London Special Services Commission, whose meeting William attended four years earlier. Their leader asked if any converted bystander would like to say something, and William did not need to be asked twice. His forceful words soon brought a crowd and the missioners realised this was someone special!

The organisers thought William would be great to lead them in holding a series of meetings in a tent on an old Quaker burial ground, around the corner from the 'Blind Beggar'. A few days later a deputation came to ask him if he would temporarily lead the tent mission. William decided to accept. This was the beginning!

The Rise of the Salvation Army

Intending to only do a week, the meetings were so successful (up to fourteen people were saved each night) that William continued there. He led two meetings each night, one in the Mile End Road and one in the tent. A report in the Wesleyan Times on the 20th August said that the people who came never usually went to church - these were the type of people that the Salvation Army would target all over the world. The report also said that they were looking for a hall to carry on the meetings in the winter.

William wrote in 'The Christian' six weeks after the start of the meetings, showing why he wanted to minister in the East End:

> "The moral degradation and spiritual destitution of the teeming population of the East of London are subjects which the Christians of the metropolis are perfectly conversant. More than two-thirds of the working classes never cross the threshold of church or chapel, but loiter away the Sabbath in idleness, spending it in pleasure-seeking or some kind of money-making traffic. Consequently, tens of thousands are totally ignorant of the Gospel and, as they will not attend the means ordinarily used for making known the love of God towards them, it is evident that if they are to be reached extraordinary methods must be employed."

Interestingly, he mentions 'moral degradation and spiritual destitution,' but does not mention economic destitution. Up to this point, William's only concern seems to be the spiritual well-being of the poor, he did not consider the poverty they lived in. His one answer was the gospel and he was extraordinarily successful in this due to the passion, sympathy and the love he had for the people. The simple and powerful way he delivered the message to sinners helped significantly.

The Rise of the Salvation Army

On July 26th William met an Irish prize-fighter, Peter Monk, walking down the street opposite the 'Blind Beggar'. He stopped to speak with him and asked him to come and hear him speak at Mile End. Monk thought William to be the finest looking gentleman he had ever seen and there was something about him that laid hold of a man. The next day he was to fight one of the best fighters, but on leaving William he believed it would be his last fight. The man he was fighting had a huge reputation and he was much bigger and stronger, but the Irishman won easily after an hour and three-quarters!

After winning he went to Mile End to hear William and a short time later he gave his life to the Lord. Peter Monk became the head of food distribution and he took meetings in the Shoreditch slums. He said that it seemed that William would tear the soul out of your body! The Irishman is just one example of thousands.

In another letter to 'The Christian', published on the 17th August William lays out his plans:

> "We have no very definite plans. We shall be guided by the Holy Spirit. At present, we desire to hold consecutive services for the purpose of bringing souls to Christ in different localities of the East of London every night all year-round. We propose holding these meetings in halls, theatres, chapels, tents, the open-air and elsewhere…We purpose to watch over and visit personally those brought to Christ, either guiding them to communion with adjacent or sympathetic churches or ourselves nursing them and training them to active labour.
>
> In order to carry on this work, we propose to establish a Christian Revival Association in which we think a hundred persons will enrol themselves at once. We shall also require some central building

in which to hold our more private meetings and in which to preach the Gospel when not engaged in special work elsewhere."

Those seem pretty definite plans and very well thought out! This is confirmed by a comment William made to Catherine on coming home after one of the Tent Meetings, "Darling, I have found my destiny". The Lord had given him the vision, and as the days went by William saw more and more of the plan until he realised that this was his destiny. At first, Catherine was not supportive, because this plan was different to the one their supporters were expecting and she worried about finance.

But she prayed and the Lord very quickly gave Catherine peace as to depending on Him for the finances. Samuel Morley, a philanthropist, had heard of the tent meetings and a month later he invited William to come and tell him all about his plans. Morley gave him a cheque for £100 (£14,000 today) which was to be his annual contribution.

Drawn to the East End by the poverty, drunkenness, immorality and blasphemy of the people living there, William had no rest until he helped them. His focusing on this form of mission lost him a lot of friends:

> "Some of them objected to his holiness teaching. Others considered that he laid too much stress upon repentance and works and too little on bare faith. Not a few grew weary of the ceaseless open-air meetings and processions with the mobbing and mockery of the crowd."

Initial Growth

In September 1865 Booth's tent was destroyed by wind and with winter coming they moved into the Dance Academy at 23 New Road, Whitechapel. Open-air meetings were held in the morning at one end of New Road: in the afternoon at the other end and in the evening on Mile End Road. Hundreds would come to hear the gospel message in the evenings and then they would walk in procession to the Dancing Academy, singing all the way. The hall was filled and people were saved. Money was a worry because the people were all so poor, but evidently, nearly every Sunday they found a golden sovereign in the box!

William wrote about this time, explaining his methods:

> "We found that though the aversion of the working class to churches and chapels was as strong as could readily be conceived, yet they eagerly listened to speakers who, with ordinary ability, in an earnest and loving manner, could set before them the truths of the Bible in the open-air. At any season of the year, in nearly all kinds of weather, at any hour of the day and almost any hour of the night, we could obtain a congregation.
>
> ...every outdoor service should, if possible, be connected with an indoor meeting, where, free from those dissipating influences which more or less always accompany outdoor preaching, especially in the streets of London, the Gospel could with greater clearness be set forth, further appeals could be made in favour of an immediate closing with Christ (also see the previous chapter), prayer could be offered and an opportunity secured for a personal conversation with the people... In this actual closing with Christ consists the only or chief ground of hope we have for sinners; without it, all mere resolutions and head knowledge will avail but little; therefore, we attach but little importance to instructing men's minds or arousing their feelings unless they can be led to that belief in Christ which results in the new creation."

The Rise of the Salvation Army

They met on Sundays at the Dancing Academy until February 1867 when they moved to the Effingham Theatre on Whitechapel Road. For week-day nights they had to use many different venues until June 1866 when they found an old wool store in Three Colts Lane that seated 120 people. The problem here was there were only low windows ventilating it and if open men would throw mud, stones and even fireworks inside. The open-air meetings were often harassed by the police, publicans and their customers. This would be the same for many years to come, even if a number of the persecutors ended up being saved.

Money was always going to be a worry for the Booths. As William's vision grew, so did the cost, and finding people to support the mission was always an important aspect of the work. Catherine became dangerously ill at this time and went to Tonbridge Wells to recuperate. On recovering they visited the home of philanthropist Henry Reed where William Haslam was speaking. That Sunday Catherine preached for him in his mission hall. The glory of God came down and Reed was very touched. They became firm friends and Reed became an important supporter of the Booths.

Another building taken was Holywell Mount Chapel in Scrutton Street, Shoreditch. The Trustees were just leaving the building having decided to close it because they had so few members, when one of them spotted William on the other side of the street. The Chairman exclaimed that William could fill the chapel, so they approached him and arranged a rent and shortly afterwards the chapel was full.

At the end of 1866, with their three venues, people could now hear the gospel all year round and William reported that they were having seventeen open-air meetings a week and twenty indoor meetings. A growing number were being saved and some good people were being raised up to do evangelistic work.

William had been very downcast by what he saw in the lives of people after they were converted. They did not become missionaries, they did not make great sacrifices, and they did not touch the lives of other people. He then realised that the one way he could lastingly change men and women was to make them, at the moment of conversion, seekers and savers of the lost.

It was not William's intention to form an organisation to look after the people once they were saved; he wanted them to join churches. Other mission movements had found it very difficult to keep their new converts and many fell away. The rough people of London did not like churches and most churches would not have them as their respectable members felt uncomfortable having them there.

This meant he was forced to look after them himself, so the new Christians were set to work immediately. They were meant to evangelise their friends and neighbours, visit the sick, hand out tracts etc.

William developed a structure to solve the problem. He insisted on a definite confession of Christ by getting people to come out to the 'penitent form' (like the altar rail). In the past ministers used an inquiry room where people who were convicted of sin could be more private and where helpers would read Bible verses to the penitent to point them to Jesus as their Saviour. William believed that a person coming to Jesus at the penitent form resulted in a much stronger Christian than one who believed that all would be well if they believed a text in the Bible. (It is likely many had an encounter with God at the penitent form). The new converts would then be watched over and instructed, trained and sent out to evangelise. This method produced long-lasting fruit.

William created the East London Christian Revival Union, which in September 1867 became The East London Christian

Mission. Two more venues were soon added which added to costs, but the Evangelisation Society heard about the work and became a generous supporter.

A newspaper report shows something of the way William reached the masses:

> "Mr Booth employed very simple language in his comments... frequently repeated the same sentence several times as if he was afraid his hearers would forget. It was curious to note the intense, almost painful degree of eagerness with which every sentence of the speaker was listened to. The crowd seemed fearful of even losing a word.
>
> It was a powerful influence that the preacher possessed over his hearers. Very unconventional in style, no doubt... but it did enable him to reach the hearts of hundreds of those for whom prison and the convicts' settlement have no terrors, of whom even the police stand in fear... He implored them, first, to leave their sins, second, to leave them at once, that night, and third, to come to Christ. Not a word was uttered by him that could be misconstrued; not a doctrine was propounded that was beyond the comprehension of those to whom it was addressed. There was no sign of impatience during the sermon. There was too much dramatic action, too much anecdotal matter to admit of its being considered dull and when it terminated scarcely a person left his seat, indeed, some appeared to consider it too short, although the discourse had occupied fully an hour in its delivery."

1867 was a year of substantial growth. Around nine more buildings, some were in terrible condition, were added in nearby areas of London, including a headquarters for The East London Christian Mission at 220 Whitechapel Road.

The Rise of the Salvation Army

This could not have been achieved without considerable support from the Evangelisation Society, whose minutes record all the money given to the various ventures of the Mission. A report during the year said that 1,000 had been converted and William now had a band of 300 helpers in his Mission.

A further report in September 1867 said that there was seating for 8,000 at a time in the various buildings and ten people working full time. Volunteers were active in house-to-house visits, where they went out in pairs, delivering tracts, speaking and praying with people and inviting them to meetings. These visitors met together weekly to support one another and to report cases of great need that they had come across. There were also four Sunday and two day schools and a Bible carriage in which two people went around selling Bibles and other religious literature, advertising meetings and preaching.

The Mission also provided reading rooms where men could get away from their rather horrid homes, into a peaceful environment to read and to fellowship with others who encouraged them to persevere in reforming their lives. The Mission also provided free food to those in particularly need, they had a soup kitchen and several mothering societies.

William was meticulous in organising the expenditure and recording of transactions. He never took any money himself, instead relying on generous people to give him enough to support his growing family.

In 1868 it was reported that one hundred and twenty services were being held every week! Many were coming to the Lord and needed to be looked after:

> "The name and address of every seeker was recorded and a ticket given to admit them to a private meeting at the Mission Hall on the following

night, when they were met by experienced and sympathetic Christians who personally examined them as to the depth of their convictions and the ground for their hope, giving suitable counsel and placing them in touch with some duly qualified brother or sister whose work it was to watch over and counsel them."

Tea meetings began to be held which became a regular activity over many years. Hundreds would come for tea and there would be a service afterwards.

William's vision was now costing £50 a week (£7,000 today) and the Evangelisation Society had to substantially reduce their giving, before they finally stopped in December 1868. By then William had created an organised institution that put it beyond the constitution of their Evangelisation Society. However, the Lord knew, and donations increased so that income just exceeded costs by the end of the year.

Publication

In October 1868, the first issue of the East London Evangelist magazine was published with William as editor. It later changed its name to the Christian Mission Magazine in 1870, to the Salvationist in 1879 and finally the War Cry at the end of 1879. To begin with, it was a sixteen-page monthly, with about 50% being articles and the rest reports from the different Mission Stations (churches). It grew in size to twenty-eight pages and in the late 1870s, it consisted almost only of reports from the Stations. By 1880 there were about 120 Stations, so it was printed weekly in order to give enough space to report what was going on all over the country.

The condition of people in the East End was as bad as ever. Near starvation, disease, lack of work – lack of hope!

The poverty and despair really tugged on William's heart, and he was desperate to help the people. He did what he could, but he knew that his primary goal was souls.

Persecution

For many years persecution was great at all the Stations. Being sworn at and mocked were the least of their problems – they had stones, eggs and mud thrown at them; tea or other things might be thrown on them from a window above where they were, or they might be hit with sticks, etc. At other times the roughs might play musical instruments or shout to drown out the preacher's voice. Policemen sometimes caused them trouble, as did publicans and magistrates. However, a surprising number of the worst offenders gave their lives to Jesus.

The missioners, many of them young women, were very brave. There are no reports of them running away or anything; they just stood at their posts, and in the end, the Holy Spirit was always the victor. It was the Mission's policy not to react to persecution and to obey the police even if their demands were unreasonable. Several times it was reported that missioners knelt down in the street in response to abuse from people.

John Allen was a navvy, and his foreman got converted and started to work on John, but progress was slow. Allen finally went to a meeting at one of the theatres because of a dare. Twelve days later he turned up to a weeknight meeting and at the end of the meeting he was convicted of sin but would not come out to the penitent form.

Knowing his situation, twenty or thirty people knelt all around him and pleaded with God for his salvation. After a long time in prayer, John began to groan and bellow like a bullock for mercy and this went on for about twenty minutes. He then jumped to his feet and shouted, "I do believe! I do believe!" The tears streaming down his face. Then he jumped up and shouted repeatedly, "The Blood of Jesus cleanses me from all sin!"

Expansion

In 1869 Catherine did a mission for several weeks in Croydon which was very successful and as a result, they were asked to form a Station there. This was the first time they had planted outside of London. Stations were often started after Catherine had a series of successful meetings.

William believed that there would be further expansion, "As rapidly as we have the right kind of worker to fill them." He recognised that such expansion would be expensive and could only be financed by people around the country with a heart to see the nation saved. Before the end of the year, new Stations were opened in Bow Common, Old Ford and Canning Town.

Despite having all these buildings for meetings, none of them was large enough for the crowds wanting to come and there were no rooms available for bible classes, believers' meetings, evening educational classes, mothers' meetings, etc. Two years earlier a building was erected on Whitechapel Road for a new venture called the People's Market, but it was a failure and in less than a year, closed. The owner wanted a lot of money for it (£3,000) and negotiations broke down, but eight months later the owner got into financial difficulties and William eventually bought it for £1,750.

It was thought to be the perfect building for evangelistic work, with several side rooms. Unfortunately, the refitting costs got out of control and an appeal had to be made to the public. Mr Morley gave £500 (£70,000 today) and someone, probably Mr Reed, gave another £500. The People's Mission Hall opened in April 1870.

Up until 1871 the Mission was completely controlled from the headquarters, but then Superintendents started to be appointed who were responsible for a designated area. By 1874 there were eight superintendents, showing how decentralised the Mission had become. It was a timely change.

In 1872 William became ill and had to rest for over six months and there was concern that there was nobody who could look after the Mission while he was sick. It was now a large organisation, with a lot of responsibilities and it had only one leader – William. Catherine had not been involved in the Mission during its first years owing to her children, her health and her taking meetings in different parts of the country. However, she knew what was going on as William involved her in discussions and many of the meetings were at her home. So, Catherine took over. She was known as 'Mother of the Army'.

In 1873 George Railton aged twenty-four joined the Mission as its secretary and became one of its main leaders. On visiting the Mission six months earlier he immediately understood the vision. He found "a real individual life which would propagate itself" and "a battalion of trained male and female soldiers, quite remarkable for their steadiness as for their readiness." He saw that money could pour into the East End from well-meaning people, but it would just be wasted unless local people worked together with God to change things.

Although the work was moving forward, it was not all good news. In Edinburgh and Brighton, there was division and they pulled away from the Mission. Sometimes the wrong person was put in charge, sometimes people just did not like the rules. No Stations were opened in 1871 or 1872, partly because the right leaders could not be found and partly because William was off sick for long periods.

In 1873, a new building was opened in Canning Town, just before the New Year, followed by new buildings at Croydon, Poplar, North Woolwich, Plaistow and Buckland. In 1874 buildings followed in Chatham, Stoke Newington, and Wellingborough. In early 1875, one opened in Hackney.

By 1876 the names of the Booth's two eldest children (out of eight), Bramwell and Katie, were beginning to appear as evangelists for the Mission. The rest would start to appear over time, although one was considerably disabled and her involvement was less than the others. William made it clear that their position in the organisation was dependent on God and their gifting, not being a child of his. In the end all but one of the children held senior positions within the Salvation Army.

Challenges

William had come up with a Constitution for the Mission in 1870, and it was revised in 1875. In it the Conference was made the final authority in the Christian Mission. It was based on that of the New Connexion Methodists. One major difference was that women were admitted to full participation, not only in the work of the Mission but also in its government. Another difference was that you were not allowed to drink alcohol if you were an officer of the Mission.

Conference was composed of the General Superintendent of the Mission (William), the secretary (George Railton), the treasurers of the Conference Fund, the life members or 'guardian representatives' (Catherine being the first), evangelists in charge of districts and two lay delegates. William had the power to do anything except over-ride Conference.

There was a lot of hope that the Constitution would work wonderfully, but the reality was that everything was decided by committee, down to deciding who should give out tracts. There was too much bureaucracy. In Conference, rules of debate were closely observed. Alterations, big or small, were made the subject of formal resolutions. Older missioners spent their time on committees instead of actively working and newcomers were put off from working because of all the red tape they had to go through.

In the twelve months to June 1876, only one Station had opened. This was Leicester, following a successful mission by Catherine.

At the end of 1876, the figures showed that the Mission stood still. William moaned that Conference was largely monopolised by "dried-up theoretical legislators." "I want the holiest and most devoted men and women to come to the front." Another reason for the lack of growth was that many of these new buildings had been financed through mortgages and they found much of their focus was on raising money to pay off the interest and capital, rather than taking advantage of the wonderful new venues.

Another disappointment was the closing of Sunday Schools because they failed the children wherever they existed. It was thought that in order to succeed there needed to be a separate organisation with staff dedicated to children's work.

Another was the failure of the soup kitchen. It worked well for a time, but then the man in charge died of overwork. The Mission slowly gave up general relief work until they stopped in 1877.

In late 1876, a deputation of the leadership went to William, saying that they were fed up with the attempted government by Conference; they had joined the Mission to serve William, so would William please take control. The Conference Committee met in January 1877, agreeing unanimously that decisions took too long, and as they were at war they needed a war council and not a legislative assembly. A new spirit flowed through the Mission.

One problem was Leicester, where the evangelist in charge had left with most of the members. A new building was acquired in February and the redoubtable William Corbridge was put in charge and the Station went forward.

William Booth was determined to press on in any way to win the lost; be it having 'Hallelujah bands' of colliers or an evangelist playing the fiddle through the streets – whatever worked, whatever the criticism. The evangelists seemed to have taken the idea of being in a war to heart. There are several reports of evangelists at different Stations saying "Victory or death" and talking of "attacking the enemy camp". (Soon, all the reports coming from all over the country, were termed in the same military language.) Sitting back was not an option.

The June 1877 Conference accepted William's proposals. He announced that nine Stations had been closed. He said that he had been in error in agreeing to the opening of these Stations. Some were in small areas that required buildings and evangelists, just the same as larger areas that had greater potential. Booth thought it best to transfer assets to areas where the fruit would be greater.

He spoke in detail on three subjects and their importance to bringing people to Jesus:

1. Hallelujah bands;
2. Holiness (the importance of this was to grow substantially over the next few years); and
3. Singing, which needed to be congregational, hearty and useful.

At Stockton, there were two converts from a brass band and they played in the procession – this was the first use of brass instruments. Another new idea was lunchtime meetings, as in the winter months the evening meetings were dark and cold.

Hallelujah Lasses

In March 1878, two women left King's Cross to take over the Station at Felling-on-Tyne. Young women in charge of Stations were soon called 'Hallelujah Lasses' and they were extraordinarily successful. The term was coined by a printer who was preparing a poster advertising the two ladies. By April 1878, nine out of thirty-six Stations were led by 'Hallelujah Lasses'.

I have not read anything about this, but I assume that the huge growth in Stations in 1877 and 1879 (from 21 to 130) was possible because of these young women who were normally under thirty, with one of the most successful only eighteen. The Mission had often had to employ its evangelists from outside its ranks, but now they were producing their own at a great rate.

The Hallelujah Lasses were extraordinary. I am not sure though how they came about; I did read that female evangelists had been used as a trial but had not really worked. I wonder if Booth was pressured into sending young women due to these passionate new Christians threatening to go out on their own, or whether it was because there were not enough men to fill all the posts in this time of extreme expansion. Then again, why women as young as seventeen? One would think that Catherine, a powerful preacher herself might have had some influence on this.

However it came about, these young women were full-blown ministers and it would be about one hundred

The Rise of the Salvation Army

years later before other denominations allowed women into that position. These young women went out two at a time, with little money to set up an organisation in an area where they knew nobody and where the people were mainly antagonistic. They had to raise money for their own living expenses and for the costs of the mission. They were mocked, reviled, had stones etc thrown at them and they were even put in prison. The workload was extremely hard and the health of many broke down to the point they either had to rest for a time or give up; some even died.

In September 1878, two young women were sent out to Consett, where they were to set up a Station. They were wonderfully successful with nearly four hundred giving their lives to Jesus in the first six weeks! That same month, a Welsh speaker was needed for Aberdare. George Railton sent Mrs Pamela Shepherd, who was the housekeeper and cook at the Whitechapel headquarters. Two weeks later she set out with her four daughters and a revival began. Some men from the Rhondda Valley begged that one of the daughters start meeting outside Aberdare, so Katie was sent to stand on street corners and preach to rough miners and a revival began. Then Katie was sent to Pentre and at seventeen she was in charge. A wonderful revival ensued with thousands coming to the Lord. It was evidently what happened here that persuaded the William Booth that women could lead Stations.

These two or three years were extraordinarily successful and it was not just with the young women. Almost wherever a Station was opened there was a move of God. Sadly, there were failures as well; Rotherham began really well, but then fell into division and the work fell apart.

Salvation Army

In 1878 there was a meeting between George Railton and William and Bramwell Booth (his son). They were discussing the cover of the Mission's report for the year that said 'Volunteer Army'. William said they were not volunteers because they felt compelled to do the work and they were always on duty. He then crossed the room and put his pen through 'Volunteer' and wrote 'Salvation' above it!

One of the Hallelujah Lasses went into the Whitechapel Hall on the morning of the assembly of the War Congress (the last Christian Mission Conference) and found a large sign being put up over the platform that said, 'SALVATION ARMY'. Congress adopted a military structure and it only lasted because the 'soldiers' agreed and supported the whole thing.

At the Congress, William instructed that no Station should go into debt without informing him. This was in response to several Stations getting into debt over their normal expenses. Any evangelist who was not happy with the new arrangements could leave and he would try his best to find them alternative work – few did.

In 1881, the General (William Booth's rank) summed it up by saying:

> "We tried for eleven years, various methods. We tried many plans... Gradually, the Movement took more of the military form, and finding, as we looked upon it, some four years ago, that God in His good providence had led us unwittingly, so to speak, to make an army, we called it an army, and seeing that it was an army organised for the deliverance of mankind from sin and the power of the devil, we called it an army of deliverance; an army of salvation - The Salvation Army."

An obvious sign of militarisation was the adoption of military ranks. So, the head evangelist at a Station would be designated 'Captain' and their number two, 'Lieutenant'. William was of course the 'General', but many had called him that for a long time as he was the General Superintendent.

While the General was fully occupied organising and directing this great expansion of the Army, Catherine was free to teach the people through her addresses and writings. The General compiled 'orders' so that everyone was focussing in the same direction as a unified force. The first publication was on, 'How to attack, capture and hold towns, together with the system which is to be carried out at every Station.' This included instructions about courting and marrying which were quite controversial and led to some calling them a sect. These rules were very similar to those of the British military at this time. But there was no change in the Salvation Army's objects – to get people to accept salvation and then turn them into evangelists.

The military system was highlighted by Catherine going around the country presenting the Corps with a banner. The Corps (new name for Station) were given numbers based on how long they had been in existence and each one received the now-famous Salvation Army flag, with the words 'Blood and Fire' on it. Catherine explains:

> "...the crimson represents the precious blood by which we are all redeemed; the blue is God's chosen emblem of purity; the sun represents both light and heat, the light and life of men; and the motto, 'Blood and Fire', the blood of the Lamb and the fire of the Holy Ghost. The flag is a symbol, first of our devotion to our great Captain in heaven and to the great purpose for which He came down and shed His blood that He might redeem men and women from sin and death and hell. Secondly, the flag is emblematic of our faithfulness to our great trust..."

George Railton wrote that flags had done more than expected in unifying the soldiers. A flag was introduced because so many people carried flags in procession that it was thought good to create one that everybody could carry. In 1882 the sun was changed to a star, representing Holy Spirit

Evangelists had long worn a sort of uniform, a dress coat, black tie, top hat etc. A leading evangelist, Elijah Cadman said, "I would like to wear a suit of clothes that would let everyone know I meant war to the teeth and Salvation for the world!" It was decided to adopt a uniform and in early 1883 a standard uniform was given out but was never made compulsory to wear.

With the huge expansion, there was a need to split the Corps into divisions and a Major would have oversight of these. At this time Bramwell Booth was the General's travelling secretary (in 1881 he became Chief of Staff) and Henry Edmonds, although a teenager was ADC to the General. This youngster was responsible for the opening of new Corps and even the firing of unsatisfactory officers. In 1881 he was given £5 and told to cover the whole of Scotland as soon as possible, despite there only being four Corps there.

The 1882 'Council of War for Majors' report said:

> "We were all deeply impressed with the appearance of that grand roomful of staff officers. Never perhaps before were so many men and women, full of such desperate devotion, bent upon the same radical plans, brought together, to spend days in consultation with such perfect love to one another and such total absence of anything whatever of an unpleasing kind. The union of mind and heart in the Army is becoming more and more astonishing in its completeness every day."

It sounds like the militarisation of the Mission achieved its goal to bring unity in relationships and purpose. It really had a positive impact on most of the Salvationists/Soldiers. They seemed to really believe that they were soldiers in a war and treated their town as a war zone, one in which it was vital to save people from going to hell. This, going to war, seems to have created much fruit in the different towns.

In 1882 "Articles of War" had to be signed by every recruit and they included a condition that the soldiers had to abstain from drinking any alcohol.

Many of the officers were young men and women, some still teenagers, yet given great responsibilities. Some officers were older and experienced in other spheres but these were sometimes unsuccessful because the person was too ingrained with what they had learned in their previous employment.

By 1886, the original eight divisions had become 85 and the rank of Colonel was introduced for officers in charge of the more important of these.

Holiness

William Booth had always been very keen on Holiness, but this increased after a conference was held on the subject to which church leaders came from all over the country. This was led by William Boardman, an American revivalist and was based on his book 'The Higher Christian Life'.

The first main article on the subject was in 1868 and when the War Cry began in 1879, there was a Holiness article every week for at least three years. Around the same time there were Holiness meetings all over the different Corps. They were about receiving the Baptism of Fire and I have read in 'The Salvationist' and 'The War Cry' many accounts of people saying that the Holiness meeting was vital for the work of evangelism. Those who received this Baptism, received more of God's power and a greater passion for the lost. The General placed it in the forefront of his teaching wherever he went, it was a major key to the success of the Salvation Army.

(My 'Baptism of Fire' booklet is available ukwells.org)

In April 1869, someone wrote about why it was so important - we really need this today:

> "This is what we are crying for in the East of London. The baptism of the Holy Ghost, and of Fire. But how much more might be done had you all received this Pentecostal baptism in all its fulness. If every soul were inflamed, and every lip touched, and every mind illuminated, and every heart purified with the hallowed flame. O what zeal, what self-denial, what meekness, what boldness, what holiness, what love would there not be? And with all this, what power for your great work? The whole city would feel it. God's people in every direction would catch the fire, and sinners would fall on every side. Difficulties would vanish, devils be conquered, infidels believe, and the glory of God be displayed."

It was Bramwell Booth's responsibility to hold a Holiness meeting every week at Headquarters, and they were very powerful:

> "The following descriptions of Holiness Meetings, taken from The Christian Mission Magazine, afford no real picture of the extraordinary sights which were witnessed, nor do they give an adequate account of the effects produced upon the souls of those who took part in them. Bramwell Booth

tells me that, after many years of reflection, and disposed as he now is to think that in some degree the atmosphere of those meetings was calculated to affect hysterically certain unbalanced or excitable temperaments, he is nevertheless convinced, entirely convinced, that something of the same force which manifested itself on the day of Pentecost manifested itself at those meetings in London. He describes how men and women would suddenly fall flat upon the ground and remain in a swoon or trance for many hours, rising at last so transformed by joy that they could do nothing but shout and sing in an ecstasy of bliss... He saw bad men and women stricken suddenly with an overmastering despair, flinging up their arms, uttering the most terrible cries, and falling backward as if dead supernaturally convinced of their sinful condition. The floor would sometimes be crowded with men and women smitten down by a sense of overwhelming spiritual reality, and the workers of the Mission would lift their fallen bodies and carry them to other rooms, so that the Meetings might continue without distraction. Doctors were often present at these gatherings. Conversions took place in great numbers; the evangelists of the Mission derived strength and inspiration for their difficult work, and the opposition of the world only deepened the feeling of the more enthusiastic that God was powerfully working in their midst."

The following article from The Christian Mission Magazine for September 1878, gives an account (edited) of "A Night of Prayer," lasting from August 8th-9th:

"The whole company, amounting to three or four hundred, settled down for the whole night, a very great advantage over meetings from which many have had to retire at midnight or early morning and from the beginning to the end, weary as almost every-one was, after four days of almost ceaseless services, the interest and life of the meeting never diminished.

Scarcely had the first hymn been commenced, when a company of butchers assembled in a yard next door, with the avowed intention of disturbing us, commenced a hullabaloo with blowing a horn, rattling of cans, and other articles, so as to keep up a ceaseless din, which was heard even whilst the whole company sang aloud. But nobody was disturbed. We felt we were fighting, that was all, and everyone seemed to sing all the more gladly and confidently, Glory, glory, Jesus saves me, Glory, glory to the Lamb.

The great object of the meeting was to address God, and it was in prayer and in receiving answers that the meeting was above all distinguished.

Evangelists came there burdened with the consciousness of past failings and unfaithfulness and were so filled with the power of God that they literally danced for joy. Brethren and sisters who had hesitated as to yielding themselves to go forth anywhere to preach Jesus, came and were set free from every doubt and fear, and numbers whose peculiar afflictions and difficulties God alone can read came and washed and made them white in the Blood of the Lamb.

That scene of wrestling prayer and triumphing faith no one who saw it can ever forget. We saw one collier labouring with his fists upon the floor and in the air, just as he was accustomed to struggle with the rock in his daily toil until at length he gained the diamond he was seeking; perfect deliverance from the carnal mind, and rose up shouting and almost leaping for joy. Big men, as well as women, fell to the ground, lay there for some time as if dead, overwhelmed with the Power from on High. When the gladness of all God's mighty deliverance burst upon some, they laughed as well as cried for joy, and some of the younger evangelists might have been seen, like lads at play, locked in one another's arms and rolling each other over on the floor.

God wrought there with a mighty hand and with an outstretched arm, so as to confound the wicked one and to raise many of His people into such righteousness and peace and joy in the Holy Ghost as they never had before, and thousands, if not millions, of souls will have to rejoice forever over blessings received by them through the instrumentality of those who were sanctified or quickened between the 8th and 9th of August, 1878.

The usual un-intoxicating wine not having been prepared for sacrament, we managed uncommonly well with water, and in fact everybody seemed to have got into a condition in which outward circumstances are scarcely noticed, and the soul feasts on God, no matter what passes outside. Under Captain Cadman's energetic leading eighty-one bore their clear simple testimony to the Blood that cleanses from all sin in a very few minutes over that time, and after a little prayer we parted."

A month later, Ballington Booth (William and Catherine's son), gives a brief (edited) description of a "Holiness Meeting," which is interesting:

September 13th was a wonderful time. Never shall I forget it. Oh, God did search all hearts that night.

After speaking about giving up all and being kept by the power of God, and singing 'I am trusting, Lord, in Thee,' we fell on our faces for silent prayer. Then God Almighty began to convict and strive. Some began to weep, some groaned, some cried out aloud to God.

One man said, 'If I cannot get this blessing I cannot live'; another said, 'There's something, there's something. Oh, my God, my God, help me. Set me straight; put my heart straight.'

Many more were smitten. Five or six more came forward. One dear man took his pipe from his pocket and laid it on the table, resolved that it should stand between his soul and God no longer. Then six or seven more came forward. Everyone was overpowered by the Spirit. One young man, after struggling and wrestling for nearly an hour, shouted 'Glory! glory! glory! I've got it. Oh! Bless God!' One young woman shook her head, saying, 'No, not tonight,' but soon was seen on the ground pleading mightily with God. Every un-sanctified man or woman felt indescribably. Three or four times we cleared the tables and (penitent) forms, and again and again they were filled.

So we sang, cried, laughed, shouted, and twenty-three had given their all to the Master, trusting Him to keep them from sinning, as He had pardoned their sins.

Never can I forget Tuesday night's Holiness Meeting, held in the Salvation Chapel, Spring Garden Lane... God backed the speaking with convicting, cutting power, after which His Spirit was poured upon us in an overwhelming manner. Immediately afterwards some twenty rushed forward for this freedom from sin. Weeping and groaning commenced in all parts, when some twenty more rushed forward. Oh, the scene at this juncture. One dear lad, not above seventeen, after lying his length on the ground for some time, cried out, 'Oh, it's come. I have it. Oh, God! my God! my God! You do cleanse me.' Then followed more wrestling and agonising, and the forms again being cleared of those who had obtained liberty.... Once more we cleared them, but only to make room for more who were waiting to come out but at this point nothing could be heard save sobs and groans and heart-rending prayers. Thus continued this mighty outpour until upwards of seventy rose testifying with feelings indescribable and unutterable joy, while all around stood weeping and rejoicing, singing and shouting.

After prevailing prayer Captains Smith, Haywood, and Coombs gave powerful testimonies of Christ's taking away and keeping from the desire of sin. I felt unutterably filled with the Spirit. Never shall I forget the scene that took place when all unsanctified were asked to come forward. It seemed as if Christ said, 'What will ye that I should do unto you?' There was a cry on all sides. Some fifteen or sixteen rushed to the front. After this, over twenty more rushed forward; while those who had obtained the blissful peace stood round singing, with faces of rapture and tears of joy." More idols cast at Christ's feet; more rose feeling the liberty; more room was made for those yet seeking; more rushed forward; and while weeping and wrestling and groaning on all sides. Some nine or ten forms were cleared until over two hundred came forward seeking in an agony of soul and heart a life of purity. We finished this meeting with 250 testimonies.

Travailing Prayer

Travailing Prayer was also very important to the soldiers. From the very beginning there are stories of evangelists meeting obstacles and then getting on their knees and travailing and breakthrough would come:

> "Prayer was soon answered and every believer got filled with God, and began travailing in birth for souls; and we once more proved our blessed God true to his promise, 'When Zion travails she shall bring forth.' Backsliders have been re-claimed, sinners saved and believers sanctified."

Every Corps would regularly have 7.00am Saturday 'Knee-drill' (prayer meetings) which were essential before going to minister on the streets, and this would have involved Travailing Prayer:

> "The prayer meetings on the Saturday nights are glorious times. The spirit of prayer prevails. What strong cries for souls! what pleadings of the promises sealed with the all-prevailing blood! what wrestlings for the salvation of sinners! what assurance of faith, mixed with shouts of Amen! Glory! Hallelujah! and Praise the Lord!"

The above accounts show clearly why the Baptism of Fire and Travailing Prayer are absolutely crucial today. The one takes away the desire to sin and allows God to empower and promote; the other pulls down the plans and purposes of the Father from heaven to earth.

I do not believe that revival will come without them!

Discipline

The first issue of the War Cry announced the reduction

in the ranks of four officers. One for getting engaged without permission, one for misbehaving in the presence of the enemy and two were guilty of light and frivolous conversation. Keeping discipline must have been hard during this time of growth. There were 120 officers in 1878 and eight years later there were 3,602!

Officer training started in 1880 with the provision of a residential building for potential female officers, which was supervised by Emma Booth (William and Catherine's daughter) and the following year there was a similar building for training the men, which was supervised by Ballington Booth. The idea was to test the genuineness of the candidate, teach the outlines of Bible history and theology, including reading, writing and spelling (many had received little education), teaching home and personal habits, train them in street work, house to house visits etc, develop and encourage devotion to God. By 1882 over four hundred cadets had been sent out as officers.

Over the next few years training expanded until the norm was for the cadets to receive six months of training, three months in the residential home and three months in the field. By June 1886, two thousand six hundred cadets had been trained.

The huge expansion at the end of the 1870s meant that there were many more exciting things to report about in 'The Salvationist'. At virtually every new Corps a revival occurred that needed to be reported, but the magazine was too small to report everything and there were complaints from the different Corps that they were being ignored. There was a desire to move to a weekly newspaper earlier, but everyone was so busy that they had no time to do it. Eventually, the weekly War Cry was published in late December 1879 until October 1882 when it went twice weekly. It had an average circulation of 200,000.

Money

Financing this growing organisation was a very difficult task. The General was in control of this at this time. He had a great instinct for the subject, and he also employed good people, but he would only take their advice when it matched his instinct on the subject. Bramwell Booth, as Chief of Staff, took over a great deal of the responsibility as he had been trained to a degree in business matters. However, he admitted that he and his father had little experience or knowledge of the decisions that had to be made, and he often had to study first-hand the questions on which they needed information.

Every Corps aimed to be self-sufficient, although this would include raising money from outside. The amount of giving by people who were very poor was exceptional. Each Corps was to give ten percent of their income to run the divisional oversight. Four times a year the offerings from a Sunday and a weekday meeting would go towards training, overseas work and the general spiritual fund. Some of the larger projects, such as the purchase of buildings could not have been done without the generous gifts from philanthropists.

The General sometimes preferred to buy buildings as it relieved the Army from significant rental costs, but he also recognised that renting had its advantages in that if the venture did not work the building could be given up, as it could be if they outgrew the venue. (This should be noted today. A church should always be growing or it is unsuccessful, so if a building is bought, one would always be selling it and buying a bigger one). Probably due to the General's vision being so big, from time to time, there were serious shortfalls in money, but appeals to the wider Christian body always brought in the required money.

Such growth at home and abroad required many new buildings. There were two fads a few years earlier, ice skating and the circus and many buildings went up to house these activities, but ice skating soon lost popularity, as did housing circus's away from the big tent. This meant that the Army was able to get hold of many of these buildings on the cheap and most of them would hold three thousand people. The Army also needed a new Headquarters which they moved to Queen Victoria Street, London and a training centre and conference hall, which they found in Clacton.

In December 1884, 'The Times' wrote:

> "The management of the Salvation Army bears witness to a method and shrewdness in dealing with circumstances which would have secured the prosperity of a commercial undertaking... As a business, the movement has beyond doubt been excellently conducted."

In 1886, George Railton wrote:

> "Over all the twenty-one years no creditor had been left without full satisfaction of its claims."

I think it is difficult to imagine the pressure the leadership must have been under for years to meet its financial obligations month by month. The number of buildings that were needed was huge, not just for all the Corps, but for training, for administration and for housing. There was only one way to deal with these pressures – on their knees. God was their provider.

Their situation reminds me of that of Holy Trinity Brompton and the enormous expansion of the Alpha Course. Their vision was constantly greater than their income, but God always provided because it was His vision too.

As mentioned, they gave up Sunday Schools because they did not want to make the children scholars, but soldiers. The 'Little Soldier' publication, started in 1881 and in its first issue said that the object of every meeting to do with children was salvation. There were different attempts to organise the children, but nothing worked until 1886 when they divided the children into companies, with an adult sergeant in charge and a sergeant-major over all the companies.

In 1884 a new work was begun as a result of the awareness of the way people lived in the city slums. It was decided that cadet volunteers from the training homes would go out in teams for no more than a month, to live amongst the people in the slums. They were called the Cellar, Gutter and Garret Brigade. They would spend each day going from house to house, washing the children, scrubbing the floors, nursing the sick, listening to problems; they took God, salvation and hope into these sad places. In the evening they gave out tracts and spent time talking to people about their souls.

Music

Having seen how playing musical instruments attracted crowds, the General encouraged every officer and soldier to learn how to play one. A February 1881 article written by Booth in the War Cry had an accompanying cartoon of someone holding a tambourine. People took up playing different instruments, but it was the tambourine that was most popular, with 1,600 being sold in six weeks.

For a long time William Booth was of the opinion that solo singing was best because you could clearly hear the words - it was a number of years before he understood that congregational singing was just as powerful. Hymns were called songs to get away from any connection with a church building, and Salvationists started to compose their own 'war' songs, many of which became very popular. Someone wrote:

> "Hymns under all circumstances have been meat and drink to me, but the Salvation Army songs have tapped a new mine. I have felt like an old warhorse hearing the trumpet sound at mass meetings. My whole being has been stirred by the power and intensity of these wonderful compositions."

The first brass band used in the Salvation Army was that of a father and three sons in Salisbury. When a new Captain visited the Fry family in 1878, he found that they were all expert musicians and he asked them if they would come and play at the meetings in order to drown out the mob who were prone to singing popular songs to interrupt the speakers. Their concerted playing quickly solved the problem. When William Booth went to hear for himself he asked the Frys' to play at some select meetings to test the water. The experiment was so successful that brass bands were immediately added to the Army's methods to attract people. Two years later a big drum was added and then a second cornet.

The head of music at the Salvation Army wrote of Fry senior, following his death in 1882:

> "I have never known a man who left behind a better report of the saintly life... and the Holy Spirit put His unquestionable seal upon all his labours... How gracious God has been by putting at the head of our musical forces a man so good, so gifted, so triumphant in a holy life of splendid service in the Army."

To begin with, the General supported Baptism and Communion but later dropped them as he did not believe them crucial to Salvation. Catherine Booth and George

Railton were the main forces behind this, believing that people could be deceived into thinking that they can be saved by going through a ceremony instead of an inward change of heart.

Instead of formal baptism, there was baptism of the Holy Spirit. In place of infant baptism was a dedication service. With Communion, the Bible indicates that Jesus wanted people to remember him whenever they ate, but taking wine was dangerous for all the ex-drunkards at the meeting. When deciding who could take Communion and who could not, a division could occur.

They also did not believe that the use of a building for spiritual purposes gave the building some sort of special sanctity.

Denominations

By 1881, the Church of England was generally mostly supportive of the work of the Salvation Army, as were other denominations. There were many reports during moves of God that denominations offered their buildings for services. This is probably because they saw them as no competition. In many instances, a significant proportion of people being saved joined other local churches, and most of them realised that the Salvation Army was targeting the roughs, who denominations had tried embracing for centuries, but never succeeded. Churches generally recognised that the Army was full of passion and energy and that they could reach the hearts of the working classes.

The Bishop of Durham in 1882 said:

> "...Whatever may be its faults, it has at least recalled us to this lost ideal of the work of the Church - universal compulsion of the souls of men. A year earlier 'The Christian Week' said, 'Underneath

their rough and forbidding exterior we discover a type of Christianity so bright, so heroic and so pure that it puts to shame the cold and fashionable Christianity of those who are pronounced in their condemnation."

There were even talks on ways the Church of England and the Salvation Army could ally with each other, but the differences were insurmountable, not least the military system the Army had adopted. As far as the General was concerned, union with the Church of England would not help in reaching the working class, they did not want to be linked in with the ceremonial aspects and they could not burden the Church with responsibility for their actions.

With the breakdown in discussions, the Church of England started the Church Army, copying the Salvation Army's methods to get to the unsaved. A few vicars were already trying to do something similar, but it was the Church Army that became predominant.

The Methodists also thought about a union with the Army. That may have made more sense as they had large chapels around the country and after all the Booths had been Methodists.

There were others in different denominations who endeavoured to copy the success of the Salvation Army.

Continued Persecution

Although they had a lot of support, they of course received a lot of criticism. Sadly people in the Church body who do nothing themselves, constantly feel they can find fault with people who are pouring their lives out for Jesus.

The first half of the 1880s was a time of increased persecution as more and more Corps were opened around the country. The main persecutors continued to be the publicans and brewers. The problem was that as there were 49,000 around the country, most of them very small businesses, they only had to lose a few customers to the Salvation Army before they were in financial difficulties.

There were a few really nasty altercations. In 1881 at Basingstoke, the Horse Artillery had to be used to quell the mob. The open-air meetings and processions were attacked, as were the homes and places of business of suspected Army sympathisers. In the same year, the leaders at Reading were nearly killed.

The following year was the 'Sheffield Riot'. A large procession that included William and Catherine Booth, was, according to the newspapers, attacked with savage ferocity. A Salvation Army officer who was on a horse was badly hurt and remained unconscious for hours; he never did fully recover. Also, in 1882 there were brutal attacks on the Salvationists, with the wife of a Captain knocked down and kicked until she was unconscious and another Salvationist was killed.

In 1882, 669 soldiers and officers were knocked down, kicked or otherwise brutally assaulted, including 251 women and 23 children aged under 15.

In 1884 in Worthing, the Salvationists were attacked for weeks. At one point the troops were called in and the Riot Act was read out. The Corps' landlord's shop was almost destroyed. Another day the mob was planning to attack an open-air meeting, but there wasn't one, so they went along the coast to Shoreham by Sea, smashed all the windows of the Corps' hall there and Captain Sarah Broadbent was killed by a flying stone.

Sometimes the publicans and brewers would employ gangs of 'roughs' to attack, harass and mock and there would be mayors or magistrates involved, in which cases the Salvationists did not get any protection from the law. These corrupt people would use their power to get Salvationists fined or put in prison. Often the accused would refuse to pay their fines as they knew that they were innocent of the charges and so they ended up in jail.

One such tragic circumstance was the wonderful Captain Louisa Lock, who led a revival in Pentre, South Wales. She and four men knelt to pray in the street and they were arrested and fined for obstruction. They refused to pay the fine and were put in jail. She was jailed for just three days, but she had a weak constitution, caught a disease there and died eighteen months later.

Some cases were appealed and higher Courts found for the Army. Eventually, the number of decisions in their favour persuaded the town mayors to stop bringing court actions, but not before many injustices had occurred. During 1884, no fewer than 600 Salvationists were incarcerated.

International Expansion

This was also a period of expansion overseas. America was targeted in 1879, Australia in 1880, France in 1881, Canada and India in 1882, and Switzerland, Sweden, New Zealand and South Africa in 1883.

From November 1884, the 'All the World' magazine was published aimed at overseas Corps.

In May 1886 there was the first International Congress. The General announced that in the nineteen countries, there were 1,552 Corps (compared with 21 in 1877), 3,602 officers, 28,200 meetings were held weekly and that buildings offered seats for 526,000 people.

'The Times' said:

> "For good or for evil the Army has taken full root as a national institution... the day has long gone by when the prophecy that the Salvation craze would subside as rapidly as it rose has been falsified by events. The Salvation Army is an established fact and it wields an immense power all over the world."

The Salvation Army had globally arrived.

Social Action

The big question we are left with is - how did the Salvation Army stop evangelising and seeking holiness? How did it lose the "Blood and Fire"?

William Booth was a man of huge vision and energy and I expect he would have evangelised the world if he could. Sometime in 1888, he was terribly impacted by seeing homeless people sleeping in the snow and living under bridges. This drove him in a new direction – social action. Up until then there had been some practical help, providing food for the poor for instance, but he had stopped it because he wanted all his financial and human resources focused on bringing in the lost.

But now everything changed, all his immense energies went into formulating a plan to permanently change the physical condition of the poor. There were lots of charities pouring food, clothes etc into the poor areas, but the people were still left poor. William wanted to change their condition for good and pull them out of poverty.

What really triggered this change I do not know. Perhaps it was the homeless, or maybe it was the fact that his wife, Catherine, was going to die, having just been diagnosed with breast cancer. Catherine's died in October 1890, aged 61.

The loss of his beloved wife was huge. Catherine had been incredibly influential in all that William did, and without her it is questionable if the Salvation Army would have existed. She was extraordinary.

Without her William immersed himself in his social scheme and two years later published a detailed plan in the form of a book called, 'In Darkest England and the Way Out'.

It sold 10,000 copies immediately and created enormous interest. It was a blueprint of what the Salvation Army was to become.

However, as had been the case for years, there were a few influential people who were directly opposed to William and his work. He was accused of many things. Unfortunately, being an autocratic leader, he opened himself up to a lot of criticism. In his book he said he needed £100,000 to start working on the vision and within four months he received £108,000. His opponents, including The Times, spread rumours that he was taking the money for himself and the family and some harm was undoubtedly done to his and the Army's reputation.

William never answered criticism, however unjust it was, but he did organise an independent committee to look into all financial affairs, including his own. It reported that everything was as it should be and that William did not and had never taken a penny from Salvation Army finances.

What an incredible achievement the creation of the Salvation Army was! William and Catherine Booth were extraordinary people. We so need a similar spiritually focused organisation to rise up today!

Summary

I end with a summary of why the Salvation Army was so successful:

- William Booth was an inspirational leader and organiser and, together with Catherine's exceptional gifts they created the Salvation Army and drove it forward.
- They made ALL decisions through Holy Spirit.
- Travailing Prayer was their main weapon to bring spiritual breakthrough before they went out to evangelise or before they made a strategic move to take on a new venue, open a new Corps, etc.
- Holiness, (the Baptism of Fire) was their second main weapon to give each person more power to attack the enemy with.
- They ignored church buildings as their target audience did not like them, so offered a host of different venues.
- They targeted a group that was not being reached by the churches and went out into the streets to gather them in.
- The evangelists were taught to speak simply and directly to the people in a way that they would understand. They put aside Christianese language.
- As in all revivals, the power of Testimony was enormous as the new converts spoke to their friends in the streets about what God had done for them.
- They marched through every street in the town regularly, so that every person in the town would be aware of their presence and message (later playing musical instruments). In most towns, thousands would gather around to listen to the message. I do find it disappointing

though that so many heard the message, but so few, relatively, responded. I would like to understand this.
- They marched people back to the venue where it was easier to preach and easier to pray for the people. A big venue, to cope with the crowds, was vital for the ministry, wherever they were. Nearly all Corps reported one thousand or thousands attending Sunday night service.
- They insisted on people admitting their sin, repenting immediately and making a decision for Christ there and then.
- Rather than making a decision for Christ through reading Scripture, their aim was for people to understand in their hearts that Christ was the answer and most would have an encounter with God in the process. This was vital for a solid faith.
- They had a good system for following up and looking after new converts. They visited people house to house, provided food, evening classes, reading rooms, etc.
- They encouraged the new converts to immediately speak out about their conversion and in doing so many became instant evangelists.
- They had a very successful model (the points above) and they had military discipline so that everybody did exactly the same. Just as in the army, each person knew the role they had and performed it. This enabled their success to be replicated across the world and splits and disunity were rare.
- The converts were instilled with such a passion, were so committed to seeing others saved and, possibly because of the Army ethos, they were so unified in their purpose, that they would do anything to achieve their goal. They would

go out in all weathers and undergo extreme persecution to take the Gospel message to the people.
- The development of the Hallelujah Lasses was extraordinary. Young girls facing a mob of working men is an amazing picture. They also helped the Public Relations of the Salvation Army.
- In the early days, they knew their target audience was the rough men and the poor, so nearly every Corps was put near a mine, port, etc.
- They underwent great persecution from roughs who were normally hired by publicans and brewers, and in places by the police, but they never reacted, often went to their knees. Many who came to mock and abuse were saved.
- Children were not ignored; they had their own services and own magazine.
- The monthly/weekly/bi-weekly magazine was full of revival reports and was used to stir up the comfortable.

Before finishing I should point out that in my opinion, it was not just the Salvation Army model that brought it huge success. The enormous growth periods seem to coincide with an awakening atmosphere being over the land. There is still more research needed into this, as it is not something that I have seen mentioned in history books so far. It seems that the Lord was doing something very special over the United Kingdom between 1858-1885, something which D. L. Moody also benefited from during his visit here 1873-75.

Having said that, the Salvation Army seems to have been the only organisation (other than D. L. Moody) that took advantage of what the Lord was doing. Did William Booth and others recognise what the Lord was doing and stepped into it, or was he just obeying the word of God?

I guess it does not matter. Whatever his reasoning, William Booth created an organisation that benefited millions across the globe, both spiritually and physically and I thank God for him.

There is a lot here for our churches today to learn from as we prepare for revival.

The main source was 'The History of the Salvation Army', by Robert Sandall, Volumes I and II.

Copies of the various Salvation Army magazines 1868-1882.

'William Booth, founder of the Salvation Army', by Harold Begbie.

'Catherine Booth, the Mother of the Salvation Army', by Booth-Tucker.

Chapter Seven

The Welsh Revival
1904-05

The spiritual state of Wales before the 1904-5 revival was not good; though it was a lot better than it is today! For the previous twenty years or so there had been new theologies springing up following the release of Darwin's book, 'the Origin of the Species'. The truths of orthodox theology were put away and replaced by liberalism which had deep roots in the universities of the day. So many of the new ministers were expounding this nonsense just before the revival. However, on this occasion, God was to show up in a mighty way and halt liberalism in its tracks. Oh, how we need Him to come and do the same thing again in our time!

There were signs that God was starting to move as early as 1900. There was a considerable amount of prayer going on around Wales in what were known as prayer circles. You can almost see how the Lord was getting His pieces on the board ready to move them when the time was right. Apart from the prayer circles there were several future leaders who were getting into position. The first was W. S. Jones who came back to Carmarthen from America in 1898. He was a Baptist minister who was transformed by two encounters with God in which he had a 'deep understanding of the holiness of God and the fire penetrated his whole nature.' This was the Baptism of Fire and those I have read about who experienced this went from being ordinary preachers to extraordinary ones, having a passion to save souls.

In 1900 W. W. Lewis, a Calvinistic Methodist moved to Carmarthen and joined up with W. S. Jones and Keri Evans, a Congregationalist, to regularly pray together to deepen their spiritual lives. In August 1903 the three of them went to the first Keswick Convention in Wales, where the teaching was about the need for a second Baptism, sanctification and holiness. Three other leaders of the revival were also there: R. B. Jones, O. Owen and Seth Joshua. All of them either before, during or after the Convention received the Baptism of Fire.

God had prepared at least eight leaders with the Baptism of Fire so He could send them across Wales as flaming arrows, setting the country on fire!

In the summer of 1903, there was a definite sign that God was on the move. In the spring four teenagers at the Pencoed Baptist church had begun meeting to pray on top of a hill. Slowly, others joined them until by the summer the church and the surrounding area were caught up in a revival.

Meanwhile, Joseph Jenkins, the minister at Tabernacle Calvinistic Methodist church in New Quay, was very unhappy with the decline in spirituality in Wales in general and in himself in particular. He recognised that his preaching was not good enough and it did not have the results he hoped for.

He then spoke to one of the ministers who had been to the Keswick Convention and learned about the blessings that many had received there. He then met up with W. W. Lewis who had experienced the Baptism of Fire. Meanwhile, he spent hours in prayer to find a breakthrough that would change him. He would soon light the main fire:

> "He refused to lose his grip on His Lord until He had blessed him, and indeed he was blessed for

he was clothed with strength from above, and he knew it. And then, when he rose from his knees a strange blue flame took hold of him until he was almost completely covered. It rose, as far as he could gather, from the floor of the room and billowed up, encircling him."

Jenkins set up a series of five conferences to help deepen the spiritual lives of people. He had received the Baptism of Fire and the first conference was held in his church, in January 1904. Nearly two months later, after the Sunday evening service, a young woman called Florrie Evans followed Jenkins home and said that she really feared the domination of the world in her life and longed for peace and joy. Jenkins told her to acknowledge the Lordship of Christ over her life. The following Sunday there were sixty at the young people's meeting and Jenkins asked them to give a testimony of their spiritual experiences. After a moment Florrie Evans rose to say, "I love the Lord Jesus with all my heart." The Spirit of God descended, the whole meeting was reduced to tears and two more young people declared their faith in Christ. This I believe was the beginning of the 1904 Welsh Revival. The young people were on fire and they went around the local churches to share the blessing.

The second conference was at Aberaeron in July 1904 and then the evangelist, Seth Joshua arrived in September and wrote, "I found a remarkable revival spirit... I have never seen the Holy Spirit so powerfully manifested." Over that week the revival was in full flow, but it needed the evangelist to add fuel for it to become a raging fire.

Back in the summer some students from Dowlas were holidaying at New Quay and after experiencing the revival took it back home with them. In July and August a big revival burst out in two Baptist churches in Pen-y-Darren and Dowlais. The pastor of the former recollected:

"I convened a special Sunday evening service for young people who desired to possess a deeper spiritual life. The Holy Spirit came down and took possession of that meeting and overwhelmed us all with power from on high. On another usual Sunday evening service the Spirit descended in the same remarkable manner; I could hardly speak, so manifest was the presence of God. There was such power in the words I spoke that strong men were broken in pieces. That night several young men gave themselves to the Lord."

From New Quay, Seth Joshua went to do a four-day conference at Newcastle Emlyn. Here, at a school for men training for ordination, were two leaders of the revival, Sidney Evans and his friend Evan Roberts. Many received salvation during these meetings and Sidney Evans was baptised in Holy Spirit. Overlapping these meetings was the third Jenkins conference which was being held for two days at the Calvinistic Chapel, Blaenannerch. Several of the New Quay young people travelled to take part in both conferences.

W. W. Lewis spoke on the first day in Blaenannerch and Evan Roberts, who was there, felt an anticipation that the fire would fall. At the 7.00am meeting the following day Seth Joshua (who had come across at the end of his conference) closed the time in prayer and included a request for God to 'Bend us'. Roberts was significantly impacted by those two words.

At the 9.00am meeting, Roberts knew he had to pray. He kept asking Holy Spirit when he should pray. As different people took it in turn to pray, the pressure built up in Roberts until he burst out. "Bend me! Bend me! Bend us!" Speaking about his experience that morning, he said:

> "It was God commending His love that bent me... Then the fearful bending of Judgement Day came to my mind and I was filled with compassion for those who must bend at the judgement, and I wept... I felt ablaze with a desire to go through the length and breadth of Wales to tell of the Saviour."

Evan Roberts had for years been in travailing prayer and had experienced many amazing encounters with God. Here I believe he was experiencing the Baptism of Fire like most of the other leaders of this revival.

A week later, on October 6th Roberts said to his friend Sidney Evans:

> "I had a vision of all Wales lifted up to heaven. We are going to see the mightiest revival that Wales has ever known – and the Holy Spirit is coming just now. We must get ready. We must have a little band and go over all the country preaching. Do you believe that God can give us 100,000 souls now?"

Over the next few weeks Roberts felt that he needed to go back to his home church, the Calvinistic Methodist, Moriah Chapel, Loughor. On Monday, October 31st the principal of the school gave him permission to return to evangelise the lost.

On his arrival his family noticed the change in him, even the way he talked was different. His brother Dan told him that his eyes were very weak, but Evan prophesied that they would be healed and they were. He sat down at the organ and began to play, but he burst into tears and said "Dan, you shall see there will be a great change in Loughor in less than a fortnight. We are going to have the greatest Revival Wales has ever seen." He then got permission to hold his meetings and the first one, with seventeen young people, was held that night.

Roberts told of what had been happening in New Quay and Newcastle Emlyn and asked them all to make a public confession of Christ. It was a hard meeting as the young people had to overcome their familiarity with Roberts and the traditions of the day. He pressed in and after a long time they each made a confession, including his brother and three sisters. It was noticed that he had changed, in that he used to be shy and nervous, but now he came to meetings with boldness and confidence. This victory, like most victories, did not come without contention. Satan invaded Roberts with doubts about his abilities and his right to lead the meetings.

The following day the meeting was at Pisgah where some of those at the meeting the previous night testified to how changed they felt after their public confession. The confession seems to have opened their hearts to the work of Holy Spirit. Six more made open confession that night. The meeting lasted three hours and consisted of confession, prayer and testimony. The training Roberts had received over the previous weeks bore fruit in these meetings, as he would only do what Holy Spirit was bidding. This was also a feature of the coming meetings.

The format of the meetings was a reading, a hymn, prayers and then Roberts would talk about

1. If there is sin or sins hitherto unconfessed, we cannot receive the Spirit. Therefore, we must search and ask the Spirit to search.
2. If there is anything doubtful in our lives, it must be removed – anything we were uncertain about its rightness or wrongness. That thing must be removed.
3. An entire giving up of ourselves to the Spirit. We must speak and do all He requires of us.
4. Public confession of Christ.

The meetings continued with some success and the word got around the neighbourhood that the Spirit was stirring. The meeting on the Friday was the largest so far, with old as well as young, Baptists as well as Congregationalists, joining the Calvinistic Methodists. The meetings became a topic of conversation, with some criticising the new method and some Roberts' state of mind. The power of the Spirit in the meetings was becoming stronger and the Saturday meeting lasted for over five hours. Sixty confessed Christ at the Sunday meeting and it was here that he taught them the prayer 'Send the Spirit now, for Jesus Christ's sake.'

By November 7th, the start of the second week; people in the town were convinced that some irresistible power was gradually taking hold of the people. At 7.00pm there was a prayer meeting and the chapel was filled to bursting. After speaking on the last chapter of Malachi, Roberts asked some of those who had not made a public confession of Christ, to do so. After a number had complied with his request, nearly everyone was moved to tears and many cried loudly and wept in agony:

> "Those present this night have no doubt that they heard some powerful noise, and felt the place filled with the Divine Presence. The people one after the other fell in agony, because of their souls' condition... The next step is more wonderful still. Evan Roberts asked them to pray the 'Direct Prayer,' as he calls it. 'Send the Holy Spirit now, for Jesus Christ's sake.' He prayed it firstly, then everyone in the meeting was to pray it in turn. When it was about half-way the second time, the whole audience gave way before some irresistible influence, and now the state of things is beyond any description."

The meeting went on for eight hours.

The Tuesday meeting was very hard. Many left early then Roberts called together those remaining. After a considerable struggle, Holy Spirit descended and he got home around 7.00am. He was awakened at around 11.00am with his mother screaming out that she was dying. She had felt so bad about leaving the chapel before the end of the meeting that Evan helped her in prayer until she found peace.

On the Wednesday Roberts was invited to hold the service at Brynteg Congregational Chapel, Gorseinon and Holy Spirit broke out there. He was in the same place on Thursday night, and it was a very powerful meeting with people coming from further afield. For the first time a reporter from the Western Mail was at a meeting. The newspaper reported that shops were closing early to ensure that the owners got a seat and the tin and steel workers were arriving in their work clothes. They went on to cover virtually every meeting for some weeks and covered them very sympathetically.

Some students from Ammanford came to one of the meetings, caught the fire and started meetings at Bethany Chapel. The fire was not of the same intensity, so they invited Roberts to come.

On the Friday the meeting was held at Moriah Chapel, Loughor again and over 650 attended, including several ministers from surrounding districts. On Saturday a long article was published in the Western Mail that was very sympathetic to what was happening in the meetings. This article brought about an invitation from a chapel in Aberdare for Roberts to preach on the Sunday; an invitation he accepted.

By now prayer meetings were being held in some houses in Loughor all day long. Two girls went to hold open-air meetings near some public houses in Gorseinon and a few young people went to evangelise some gypsies who had encamped near Loughor. In both places there were salvations.

That night the new chapel at Moriah was filled long before the time to begin the service, so Roberts asked his friend Sydney Evans, who had just returned from Newcastle Emlyn, to take the overflow into the old chapel. However, in minutes that was full as well. Several of the people there that night had come to scoff but ended up giving their lives to Christ. It was past 5.00am when the people went home.

During these two weeks the fire was burning in other parts of Wales. Joseph Jenkins had a good deal of success with his meetings and arrived at Ammanford to find the fire that had started beginning to wane. After a series of meetings the fire rekindled and when Seth Joshua arrived on November 19th the fire burst into flame. Another flame of the Revival was in Tonypandy in the Rhondda. Holy Spirit had been stirring since the beginning of 1904 at Trinity, an English speaking Calvinistic Methodist chapel (the other chapels so far mentioned were all Welsh speaking). By October six hundred had given their lives to Christ.

The reporting of the meetings in the Western Mail is why Evan Roberts is known as the face of the revival. At 26, single and not tied to a church like most pastors, he was a very attractive figure as far as the press were concerned. The more they wrote about him the more invitations he got and the more famous he became. However, that he was not really doing anything more than many others, except he had the freedom to visit wherever he wanted.

North Wales

Early in 1904, Rosina Davies held a successful mission in Rhos, North Wales. The beginning of a revival started in June in the Baptist church at Ponciau just half a mile away.

The Welsh Revival

On November 8th, when Roberts was just into his second week of meetings, R. B. Jones began a ten-day mission here. R. B. Jones had been baptised with Fire after the Keswick style convention and had been travelling around the country teaching mainly on holiness. Before his experience with God he was considered a very good preacher, but afterwards he was an exceptionally powerful one.

God had prepared the ground, so the revival broke out immediately and spread around the district. As with Roberts, R. B. Jones was always led by Holy Spirit. The Rhos meetings were also covered by the press. So you see, God prepares the ground, often over a large area – in this case the whole of Wales and it is up to us to recognise what He is doing and step into it.

Here is a wonderful, edited, personal account of a churchgoer who found Jesus, like so many thousands of others:

> "One Sunday evening in our church, as November was drawing to a close, an announcement was made that Siloah Congregational Chapel was open daily for such meetings as the miners on the night shift cared to attend. A meeting for the miners at such a chapel was certainly a novelty, but all were warmly invited. I thought it would be a novelty to attend, especially if these illiterate miners - as many of them were reputed to be - would make known their experiences in the revival. At that time the town was only partially influenced by the revival - the floodtide came later. The twenty-third of November proved to be my day of destiny. Little did I dream that there lay buried in that unobtrusive reminder a veritable revolution.
>
> About nine-thirty, I left my room and walked

toward the centre of the town, puffing nonchalantly at my fragrant cigar. My thoughts were heavy; an inexplicable sadness was in my heart. Reaching the end of the street I hesitated, not knowing which direction to take. Where should I go? When I was in the act of following an impulse, someone seemed to whisper, 'No, you must go straight forward.' Without more ado, I crossed the road, took the street that lay before me, and went on to my Bethel, the church where the revival services were.

Familiar revival melodies reached my ears. It seemed as if an angelic choir had come from heaven to drown earth's sorrows in a sea of song. It was marvellous! Could the singers be miners? The sweetness of the air, 'O! say, will you take up your cross? O! say will you take up your cross?' captured me. Yes, I was actually turning the little refrain over in my mind when I met a young woman, greatly agitated. She was well known to me. But what power had stirred her to the extent that she seemed beside herself? This was so unusual for her that I felt startled. Had someone molested, insulted, or frightened her? With an appealing tremble in her voice she exclaimed, 'You must come - you must come at once - you must come at once to the revival!' She pointed excitedly to Siloah Chapel, the source of the glorious music. 'It is wonderful - wonderful - in there! Come quick!' Amazement took hold of me.

For once in my life the power of speech deserted me - I simply looked on. I must have looked at her incredulously for she persisted in exclaiming, 'It is wonderful - wonderful - wonderful!' Like one in a dream, I accompanied her to the chapel - or rather, the vestry door. Again the rapture of the singing thrilled me. Such marvellous singing, quite extempore, could only be created by a supernatural power, and that power the divine Holy Spirit. No choir, no conductor, no organ - just spontaneous, unctionised soul-singing!

An irresistible attraction, resembling a tremendous magnetic force, drew us inside the vestry. All the seats were occupied, except a few right in the front. Directed by this woman, I tiptoed up the aisle to a seat. It must have been about ten o'clock and lo! the vestry was a mass of worshipers absorbed in the adoration of God. Almost as soon as we were seated, the woman slipped to her knees, breaking forth in such passionate prayer as I had scarcely ever heard, certainly not outside of the revival meetings. No one would have credited her with such eloquence. Indeed, no one had ever heard her engage in public prayer. Words poured from her lips. The power of God had overwhelmed her, and she was now overcoming. All shyness, timidity, frailty, and human weakness had vanished.

Petrified with fear, I wondered what was going to happen next. I became conscious of one thing, that I was sitting perilously near the 'fire'— nearer than ever before in my life. What could I do? Escape? Even if contemplated, that would have been an ungracious act, if not cowardly. Besides, had I not been somewhat familiar with these unearthly proceedings during my visit to the revival in Trecynon? This was only another edition - a second edition of the services which had so intrigued me in Ebenezer. This woman's prayer continued in fervency and passion. Seriously reflecting upon the situation which was momentarily developing into a spiritual crisis before my eyes, I could only indulge in a quiet, inward, mental observation: What a place is this! Everybody seemed to have been affected by this prayer, for all were engaging in intercession, without let or hindrance. One person, with a yearning for communion with God, had mightily moved this congregation heavenward. It would need more bravado than bravery for any man to have dared to interfere with this inrush of divine power.

Singing, sobbing, praying intermingled and proceeded without intermission. When this glorious commotion seemed to have reached a peak, there came through the air a small melodious voice softly singing, 'Come to Jesus; come to Jesus; come to Jesus now.' It persisted until the people joined in the sweet refrain, inviting sinners to take the irrevocable step that meant salvation. It must have commenced in one of the back seats. But all hearts were soon completely captivated. People joined heartily in the invitation which echoed and re-echoed through the building.

My poor mind was tossed about with every extraordinary manifestation of the Holy Spirit's working upon the hearts and minds of these people. Sometimes I felt like shouting; again I felt like doubting. At all times I was puzzled. There was no gainsaying the fact that the prayers of these comparatively illiterate people must have been divinely inspired; one felt convinced that simple, ordinary worshipers of themselves could never have composed such sublime sentences as were expressed. The petitions were divinely indited. Some of them fell upon my spirit like red-hot coals, and I was troubled.

My heart became heavy. Almost unaware of what I was doing, I sighed continually. The burden increased with the progress of this service until I felt myself crushed. From some part of the building came the words: 'Seek ye the Lord while he may be found; call ye upon him while he is near.' Surely He was 'near' enough just then, never so near as at that moment. But the voice continued with emotion, 'Let the wicked forsake his way, and the unrighteous man his thoughts: and let him return unto the Lord.'

I could not but feel that this call to 'return' was meant for me, although I had not the faintest idea how to 'return.' Morally there was no need for me to do so; but spiritually-ah! that was where I felt pinched and humiliated. Inwardly I was convinced that I had 'come short of the glory of God' in spite of my boasted morality. 'And he will have mercy upon him,' went on the voice; then, as if in a mighty crescendo: 'And to our God, for HE WILL ABUNDANTLY PARDON!' These words produced a great effect upon my disturbed mind.

In every prayer there seemed to be Scripture for me - I was literally 'mobbed' with the words of God. Beyond a doubt it was the ministry of the Holy Spirit 'Comfort ye my people, saith the Lord,' said another. And was I not in desperate need of some comforting word at that moment. Heavier and still heavier became the burden. Lower and still lower drooped my proud head. Sometimes I felt like falling in a heap on the floor, bewailing my state.

How it happened I do not know. Whence it came, God alone knows. It has always remained a mystery as the years have come and gone. Was it something disturbing my sub-conscious mind, flinging upon the screen of my mind a scene of gospel-days with which I had been familiar since boyhood in Sunday school? The passing of the years has produced no satisfactory answer; 'the day will declare.' The reality of it has lasted through forty-three years of the most strenuous labours in the Master's vineyard, on three continents. My soul was utterly overwhelmed with the sense of awful sin. Deliverance tarried long, while unbelief mocked. My eyes were fast closed. A panorama passed before the eyes of my mind, whether a vision or a mental impression. In those moments I saw more with my eyes shut than I had ever seen in my previous life.

There appeared a huge multitude, varied in costume but differing little in features, interested in a central Personality whose presence was the sole cause of their assembling. Moving majestically among the people, He appeared to speak words of encouragement. Suddenly, a blind beggar, staff in hand, pushed his way through the crowd, and knelt in the pathway of the Speaker crying, 'Jesus, thou son of David, have mercy on me!' Some reached to pull him out of the way, but a hand was extended to protect the defenceless man. Standing with royal bearing, the central figure encouraged the people to bring the poor fellow to Him. Again, dropping his staff and extending his hands, the beggar evidently repeated his cry.

Then something within snapped - my bonds were gone. I jumped to my feet, extended my arms, and took up the poor man's words. Oh! how I cried! Was ever such a cry heard anywhere? Desperately, passionately, fervently, I cried, 'Jesus! Jesus! Jesus!' over and over again, unable to continue with petition. With that one word, I held on like a drowning man clutching a straw - it seemed to be my last chance, absolutely the last.

'Jesus! Have mercy! Have mercy! Have mercy on me!' I cried. How many times, I do not know. This I do know that no argument of a psychological nature can ever disturb the serenity of my faith. A sweet voice spoke within my spirit so clearly, unmistakably, audibly, that the voices of all creation could never succeed in drowning its message: 'Be of good cheer, thy sins are forgiven thee.'

Heaven came into my heart that very moment... There were sins to be banished, and they were banished. There were burdens to be dropped, never to be picked up on any pretence again... No chain has since been forged that was strong enough to hinder my service for the Master or to retard the advancement of my spiritual progress. Delirious joy possessed my soul instantaneously. Henceforth there was no keeping quiet. Revival had swept shyness away. So possessed was I with the 'new wine of the kingdom of God' that I, like many others in the revival, seemed to have lost my mental equilibrium and self-control. This great miracle within me must have taken place in the neighbourhood of eleven-fifteen, as near as an estimate of the time can be made. According to that calculation, I had been in the church about an hour and fifteen minutes. It seemed to me like eternity, since the burden on my spirit had been so heavy.

Hundreds in that building felt exactly as I did. Worship according to the old dignified order was banished unceremoniously. On and on and on went that glorious miners' meeting, leaving a golden trail behind. Is it not still going on? While my heart beats, that revival service will neither slumber nor sleep. It is fadeless, endless, eternal!"

Characteristics

Some of the characteristics of the revival are based mostly upon Evan Robert's meetings as there is so much more written about him than the other leaders of the revival.

All of Evan Robert's services and many others, would have people queuing more than an hour before the service started. The people would spend the time singing hymns and talking about the revival. Often, people could not get into the church, so they would wait outside hoping to hear something or to get in later. In two towns that totalled five thousand inhabitants, there were four churches, all of which would be full of four thousand people. Remember the main part of this revival took place in mid-winter.

The Welsh singing was a major characteristic of the revival. Roberts normally arrived with one or more of the young women from New Quay who were renowned for their solo singing and the effect of their singing on the congregation was often electric.

The Western Mail states Robert's role:

> "The visits of Mr Evan Roberts and his singing evangelists appear to be merely what he himself so aptly described them, 'opening the doors' of the revival, for the work which is carried on by others is becoming vast in its extent and wonderfully effective in its operations. People who attend his meetings get 'fired' with the zeal of the revival, and proceed to the neighbourhoods in which they live and spread the 'infection' wherever they go - not only in the Churches, but in the works, in the streets, in the trains, and the subject has become, especially in the mining valleys, the principal topic of conversation among all classes of the community."

The Welsh Revival

The revival was talked about everywhere; it enveloped people's lives. Prayer meetings would pop up all over the place as did impromptu meetings, even down in the pits. Here is a short description of a meeting, again from the Western Mail:

> "The service was soon in full swing, prayer after prayer, hymn after hymn, and address after address following in quick succession. So impetuous had the participants in the work become, that before long, song and prayer were heard simultaneously."

Roberts relied as much as he could on Holy Spirit in his ministry, both as to where to preach and how the meetings were to flow. He would always pull back and not try to lead the meeting. Someone might come up to read a Bible verse, or someone might start singing a hymn or someone might stand up and pray or give a testimony and even if he was speaking Roberts would allow the interruption.

The meetings generally went on a long time as one service would often merge into the next; I read of one going on for ten hours. Even after being in church for such a long time, there were impromptu services on train platforms, or even on the trains, as people made their way home.

Roberts would often not give a sermon which was quite common in the Revival. This was probably the reason why so many fell away afterwards as they were not grounded in the Word. He concentrated on telling people about the love of Jesus rather than on judgement which previous revivals had done. Someone wrote, "The only gospel promulgated is the gospel of love."

Roberts would always pray intensely but would mostly not vocalise them. He would often be seen kneeling, sweating profusely as a result of the intensity of his prayers. A witness wrote:

> "His soul appeared to be saturated through and through with the spirit of prayer. It was the atmosphere in which he moved and lived. He enjoyed uninterrupted intercourse with heaven. Whenever one looked into his face, he seemed to be engaged in intercession. It was an object lesson to all. Prayer was the breath of his soul."

Often repeated phrases used by Roberts were, 'Obey the Holy Spirit' and 'Empty me, fill me, use me.' People noticed how humble he always remained despite all the personal attention on him. A witness observed:

> "We have plenty of better speakers, and, possibly, abler men, but they do not seem to be imbued with the same power as he wields in drawing these immense crowds and keeping them together. At present I can only account for it by the fact that he comes from the midst of the Loughor fire."

I would suggest that it was because of the time he spent in the presence of the Lord.

Evan Roberts meetings began to change in the new year.

The Western Mail said:

> "On the 4th Jan 1905. Roberts asked a singer to stop as he did not think he had been inspired by the Holy Spirit. He had before allowed the meetings to continue, but he said Holy Spirit had told him to stop the quenching of the Spirit by anybody and everybody who might get up."

I am puzzled by this as the meetings before New Year do not seem to be any less powerful than those afterwards.

On January 22nd Roberts had a meeting in the Congregational Church in Dowlais, where there had been powerful meetings for several months, but this resulted in a huge controversy. The pastor wrote a scathing article saying that his was a genuine revival and Roberts was fake. Roberts never responded to the attack and he had a lot of support but the accusation clearly hurt him. A few days later he retreated to a week of silence and after that, he kept pointing out 'obstacles' in his meetings. Three weeks later his effective work in the revival was over. He had meetings in Liverpool in April, Anglesey in June and North Wales in December, and then that was it. Roberts had a nervous breakdown and retired to Leicester.

So what were the effects of the revival?

There was great unity during the revival. Roberts would often have three meetings in a town in a day; each one at a different denomination. In many towns there could be three or four meetings going on simultaneously. In one place there were twelve churches and most of them would have been full each day. In Aberdare there were a dozen large meetings held in just one day.

The behaviour of the people was transformed. Many pubs closed down and many more had a significant decline in their business. People would sometimes order a drink but then leave without touching it because of the presence of God all around. There was therefore little drunkenness, little swearing and little crime generally – magistrates had hardly any cases to try. Old debts were paid off, bad relationships were healed, theatres and sporting events suffered as people wanted to be praising God instead.

Although much time was taken with prayer and meetings, employers noticed a much-improved work ethic. The presence of God invaded everywhere – schools, colleges, the streets, etc. I love one story where a young girl asked,

"Teacher, are you saved?" and the teacher fell on the floor, gave her life to Christ and became a missionary. As with most revivals it produced the next generation of pastors and missionaries.

R. B. Jones wrote:

> "If one were asked in a word the outstanding feature of those days one would unhesitatingly reply that it was the universal, unescapable sense of the presence of God... It mattered not where one went the consciousness of the reality and nearness of God followed."

This has been true of every revival; it is the key.

Like many of the big revivals, this one was not confined to Wales because God was moving across the world; although mainly because most of it was in the Welsh language, it sadly did not spill into England. The intensity of the revival was only four months, November-February, which is surprising. Evan Roberts believed and prayed for 100,000 salvations, but my own calculations based on dozens of newspaper reports show at least 130,000 were saved. It must also be remembered that the following year the Lord broke out in Azusa Street, a revival that has led to more than 100 million Pentecostals around the world!

The 1904 Welsh revival was wonderful and we need one desperately today, but this time we need ten million plus coming to Jesus, not 130,000.

There is a lot written about the 1904 Revival. If you want to read a detailed account of Roberts early life and his part in the revival, get 'Evan Roberts, The Great Welsh Revivalist and His Work' By D M Phillips from your library. Phillips accompanied him to many of his meetings and he includes many letters and detailed accounts of where and when he spoke. He describes Roberts in a lot of detail. The book was published in 1906.

A more concise version is 'The Welsh Revival of 1904' by Eifion Evans, published in 1969 by Bryntirion Press.

A wider account of the revival is 'Fire on the Altar' by Noel Gibbard, published in 2005 by Bryntirion Press.

Chapter Eight

The 1921 Forgotten Revival
England's last awakening

In 1921 the war had been over less than three years and times were hard in Lowestoft, Suffolk. There was little work for those who had fought for their country, except for building sea defences. Their spiritual condition was also hard. Revival had come to Norfolk and Suffolk through the work of William Haslam in the mid 1860's, but the area was hardly touched by the Welsh Revival of 1904. There were a few signs of spiritual activity, mainly amongst the young at the Fisherman's Bethel and London Road Baptist Church.

Hugh Ferguson took over London Road Baptist Church in 1917, two years later starting a prayer meeting, hoping to see a great manifestation of God's power. Up to ninety people attended this weekly meeting. Ferguson was passionate to see revival, but he wanted someone to come and set the spark. He had heard that a Douglas Brown of Ramsden Road Baptist Church, Balham, London was an anointed preacher, so he went to hear him. After hearing him preach Ferguson asked Brown if he would conduct a series of evangelical services in Lowestoft, together with Bible readings for Christians. He agreed and it was decided that he would go for a week on March 7th, 1921.

Brown's father was a pastor and was an inspiration to his son. He was happy in Balham. His church was full, he had not known a Sunday in fifteen years without a salvation and he loved his congregation. Yet one day in November he returned to the vestry after preaching and broke down. God had started to deal with him, and for four months he wrestled with the Lord. One Saturday night he wrote out his resignation to the church he loved, because he felt that he could no longer preach while he was in contention with God.

That night something happened. "I found myself in the loving embrace of Christ forever and ever, and all power and joy and all blessedness rolled in like a deluge." God had been calling him into mission work, something Brown did not want to do, but he finally gave in. Four days later he was in Lowestoft.

Brown had been suffering with flu for eleven days and was feeling very unwell, so in case he was too sick to preach, he brought with him John Edwards, a pastor from Brixton. The meetings were well advertised and the church, which held 750, was well filled for the first service on Monday evening. The following day there was a prayer meeting in the morning, a Bible reading in the afternoon and another full evangelistic service in the evening. Holy Spirit was felt in the meeting, but Brown did not make an altar call. Ferguson described the Wednesday morning prayer meeting as 'wonderful'.

On Wednesday evening Brown preached on the man at the Pool of Bethesda in John 5. Ferguson recounts:

> "We had the church packed in the evening. When our brother had delivered his message, he told the people he was going into the vestry and would be glad to see any who wanted help or desired to surrender themselves to Jesus Christ. I shall never forget that night as long as I live."

One by one they came to the vestry until there were queues going down the aisles. Because of the numbers they opened the schoolroom and the people poured in. Those who had made a definite commitment to Christ were taken to one side, and those who were experiencing difficulties were taken to classrooms where experienced Christians helped them. Sixty to seventy young people came to Christ that night.

The Thursday evening service was at the Fisherman's Bethel. The inquiry room was packed with people crying out to God within a few minutes of the end of the sermon. People came to Jesus all over the building that night. By the end of the week it was obvious that God was doing something special, so Ferguson met with two other leaders, that resulted in an invitation to Brown to return to Lowestoft on Monday, after he had conducted Sunday services at his home church.

The following week the Bible readings were held to full houses at Christ Church. Someone described the messages as 'bombshells'. The two most memorable were on 'The Judgement Seat of Christ'. These messages were aimed at the new Christians and those who, up until now, had only heard a social gospel. In the evening meetings the 'Word' predominated over everything else, and the Cross was central to every meeting. One old man, remembering those days, said, "He (Brown) was different from anybody else I heard, it was as though he was speaking to me personally." Another said, "I remember Douglas Brown preaching on the Cross and describing the nails with tears."

One evening there were so many in Christ Church that the pastor had to ask all those who loved Jesus to go into the Parish Hall to pray, so that they could fit in everyone. There were so many answers to prayers as people prayed for their families and friends to come to know Jesus. On one night a husband and wife were in different inquiry rooms, both wondering how they were going to explain to one another their new love for Jesus.

Douglas Brown saw a man on his knees outside the Fisherman's Bethel. On asking him what was going on, he was told that the man had been praying for years for his three sons and they were all in the inquiry room. A woman, whose family had recently died, was on the way to the harbour to commit suicide, when she heard singing coming from the Baptist church. She went in and the following day she gave her life to Christ. One pastor said, "There have been times when Mr Ferguson and I have gone alone and sobbed out our hearts together in joy at the great things God has done for us."

During the last week in March 1921, the meetings moved to the 1,100 seater St John's Church. The meetings were full, with people coming in from the surrounding districts. The final meeting in St John's took place on April 1st. There was great unity amongst the churches of Lowestoft; Sankey's hymns were sung as they were in most of the meetings and a wonderful celebration was held. Douglas Brown was given a tremendous send off on April 4th as he went back to his church. There was a minimum of five hundred converts recorded in the four weeks of meetings held in Lowestoft.

He returned to Lowestoft at Whitsun (May) 1921 to do a week of meetings in the villages surrounding the town. A newspaper reported that this week of meetings was even more powerful than those in March, particularly that in St Michael's Oulton. Brown had been staying at the Oulton rectory for this week of meetings, and the night before the meeting he was awakened by a voice saying, "Thou shalt see greater things than these." He went down to the study to pray, but he was soon joined by the rector who had been awakened by the same words.

From May 30th to June 3rd Douglas Brown was in Ipswich for a week. For more than a year the Free Church ministers had been meeting to pray for revival. Again, the power of

God was present and people gave their lives to the Lord. Like all of Brown's meetings, these were very calm affairs, with little emotion being shown. The Word was preached, people were led to the Cross and several chose salvation. Another feature of this time was the resolve of ministers to shepherd the converts and train them for service. At Ipswich a family of nine all came to be converted.

The following week Brown was in Great Yarmouth where the revival continued. St George's held 1,100, but over 1,500 squeezed into the meetings, with hundreds committing their lives to Christ. Then came Norwich two weeks later. St Mary's Baptist Chapel had to have extra seats put down the aisles for the first meeting to cater for the demand. As usual there had been little publication of the meetings, and there were no organising committees, but the word had got around.

As in other places Hugh Ferguson went with Brown to the meetings held in various churches. Again, many non-Christians and nominal Christians found salvation. The week of July 11th found Brown in Cambridge at the Zion Chapel. Amongst the ministers who joined with him was the evangelist, Gypsy Smith.

Early in September 1921 Douglas Brown reported:

> "A momentous revival is within the reach of the churches. In East Anglia it has commenced. Whether it becomes national depends upon the message and methods adopted by various churches during the coming winter."

During the week of September 19th, there was a conference in Lowestoft which Brown led, and the revival continued.

As the conference was ending thousands of men and women were coming to Great Yarmouth and Lowestoft from Scotland. These were the herring fishermen and the women who gutted and packed the herring for curing. They would track the shoals of herring as they headed south down the UK. Unlike the local fishermen the Scottish fleet would not sail on a Sunday, instead many of the men and women went to local churches to worship.

Amongst those travelling down from Scotland was the evangelist Jock Troup, a barrel maker from Wick. Troup was born in 1896 and although brought up in a Christian family he was a wayward young man. It was while in the Royal Navy Patrol Service in the First World War that God started His work on Troup. He recounts what happened:

> "Something laid hold on my life and I became utterly miserable. I tried to throw it off but the conviction deepened. We left for patrol the next day, Monday, and I could never explain the awful misery of that week. Day and night I was like a hunted man; my sin was before me every moment. I tried to get rid of it by resolving to turn over a new leaf, but it seemed the more I tried, the more my conscience smote me. I stopped swearing and gambling and tried to give up smoking...The burden had grown till it kept me from sleeping lest I should die and wake up in hell... (One day) on arriving at the ship however, I opened the wheel house door and got on my knees and cried to God to save me for Jesus' sake. My burden simply rolled away and the deliverance was so sweet that I rushed into the cabin to tell the crew what had happened."

In 1920 God took hold of him again to prepare him for the work Troup was to do. In 'Our Beloved Jock,' James Alexander Stewart says:

> "Mrs Troup has reminded me that the secret of all her husband's ministry was the mighty experience

that took place in 1920 in the Fisherman's Mission at Aberdeen. Something glorious happened there that made him the man he became. He entered into a definite experience with the blessed Holy Spirit. This experience was so sacred to him that he did not mention it often, and then only to a few intimate friends." (This is what I believe is the Second Baptism or Baptism of Fire which so many revivalists experienced).

Against this background Jock Troup arrived in Great Yarmouth in the autumn of 1921. On the third Saturday in October Troup stood in the Market Place and preached on Isaiah 63:1. Suddenly the power of God came down and strong fishermen were thrown to the ground and cried to God for mercy. The presence of God was there for many days to come, and many were brought under a deep conviction of sin.

On one occasion three girls from Scotland failed to turn up for work. Their employer found them in their rooms, deeply troubled in their soul. Troup was called for; he led them to Christ and they went back to work. Men were saved on their boats out at sea. One man telegrammed home to Scotland, "Saved ten miles from Knoll Lightship. Last to ring in on this ship." 1921 was one of the worst herring harvests on record, mainly because of the terrible weather, but it was a great year for the harvest of souls.

Douglas Brown returned to Great Yarmouth for the first two weeks of November, joining Troup for a few days until Troup was called away to Scotland. He had had a vision of a man in Fraserburgh who was praying for the Lord to send them the evangelist. Powerful meetings continued to be held in four churches.

The Congregational Church was filled for the morning prayer meetings. Two hundred prayer requests a day were made for loved ones. Prayers were not more than a minute long, and as the week went on, answers to previous prayers were noted with great joy.

Each afternoon around seven hundred filled the Deneside Wesleyan Church to hear the Word of God. In the evening Deneside and St Georges were jammed with 1,500 people. The presence of God was very strong. Brown said of the November 5th evening meeting:

> "I tell you frankly, if a man could pass through a meeting like that without breaking his heart with joy, he must be made of granite."

Open air meetings went on each day, despite the dreadful weather. One night between eleven o'clock and midnight, in a howling gale and torrential rain, twenty-two men went down on their knees in the wet and committed themselves to Christ. There were several amazing conversions and whole (ten men) boatloads gave their lives to Christ. At the end of the terrible fishing season the men and women of Scotland returned home to their various towns and villages, and the word spread.

Jock Troup was the forerunner back to Scotland. As soon as he arrived in Fraserburgh he spoke in the Market Place. A crowd gathered and it was suggested that he continue the meeting in the Baptist Church. On arriving at the church they found the pastor and deacons leaving. They had just finished a meeting where they had decided to invite Troup to come to Fraserburgh. Among the deacons was the very man Troup had seen in his vision.

The service had only just begun in the church when people began weeping over their lost condition. The revival had come to Scotland. There were open air meetings in Saltoun Square, and by December the only venue big enough was the 1,200 seat Parish Church.

The 1921 Forgotten Revival

While the revival was going on in Great Yarmouth, revival meetings were taking place in Wick, so when the new converts arrived back in Wick there was already a revival atmosphere. Remarkable scenes took place at the end of November with crowded meetings indoors and out, with tears of repentance and scores of converts. Early in January 1922 Troup arrived from meetings in Dundee, prolonging the revival.

The revival atmosphere came to Eyemouth as the fishermen and women returned home to Scotland. The Spirit of revival was still evident in 1931 when Troup visited the town. He spoke in the Market Place to about three thousand people, even though the population of the town was only two thousand and many gave their lives to the Lord. The word spread to many other ports along the shores of the Firth of Forth, such as Missleburgh, Fisherow and Pittenweem.

One of the fishermen who returned to Peterhead was David Cordiner. Whilst in Great Yarmouth the Lord told Cordiner that he was to preach. His friends tried to persuade him out of the idea as he was a very quiet man, but he stepped out and led the revival in Peterhead. There were meetings every night for six weeks and hundreds professed faith in Christ. Revival meetings were also held at Gardenstown, where Castle Grant Hall was packed every night, with souls being saved. Several towns along the north coast of Banffshire were impacted. In Inverallochy and Cairnbulg, within two weeks, there were six hundred conversions out of a population of 1,500.

Many places in Scotland were touched by the flame from Great Yarmouth and Lowestoft. There were many converts in Dundee, Aberdeen and Glasgow, but the revival seemed to stall sometime in 1922.

Jock Troup went to Bible School at the Bible Training Institute in Glasgow from 1922-24. However, he would always be drawn to evangelising; so much so that the Institute could not award him a certificate because he did not complete enough of the classes. He was an itinerant revivalist until 1932 when he became Superintendent of the Tent Hall in Glasgow. The Tent Hall did a huge amount of work evangelising and serving the poor. The war years took a toll on his health and he resigned in 1945. He travelled again to many parts including Canada and America. He was in the pulpit of Knox Presbyterian Church in Spokane, Washington, when he collapsed and died. A doctor had warned him that he would die if he did not ease up, but Jock often said that he wanted to die in harness.

So, England missed a large awakening because ministers did not realise the season they were in. Brown and Troup knew what season they were in and brought salvation to many people, but where were the other revivalists? Why did they not join in? If two did so much, how much would twenty or two hundred have done?

In 1921 God was on the move elsewhere in the world, including Northern Ireland through W P Nicholson. It is vital that we recognise the season we are in and step into it.

If you want to know more about Jock Troup then read 'Revival Man, the Jock Troup Story' by George Mitchell, published by Christian Focus.

Much of the above is taken from 'A Forgotten Revival' by Stanley C Griffin, published by Day One Publications.

Chapter Nine

The Hebrides Revival
The UK's last awakening
1949-54

This is probably the most famous revival that has been experienced by the United Kingdom, possibly because it is the most recent being from 1949 to 1953.

The sad thing is that the revival did not spread to the mainland. There was a good reason for this in that the quickest journey to the mainland was seven hours by boat, which made it difficult to get news of the revival out and difficult for anyone to go and experience it. Accurate accounts of the revival are few; it is a shame that nobody recorded what happened at the time. We are indebted to Mary Peckham, who was at the revival and who grew up on the Island, for her book which was published in 2004.

Background

Another mistake people make about the Hebrides revival is that it was a one-off on the island. This is far from the truth. Just before the Second World War in 1939 there was probably an even bigger revival with equally amazing manifestations and fruit. In my research, I have found that there was a revival going on somewhere on the island for forty of the fifty years prior to 1949, so the islanders would have been very familiar with the idea of a revival.

There were three denominations on the island; the Church of Scotland, the larger Free Church that did not participate officially in the revival, and the Free Presbyterian Church of Scotland who opposed it. In the 1950s virtually everyone went to church every week – the church was the centre of the community. Sundays were universally held in high esteem and set apart for God. Members of the church all attended weekly prayer meetings. These prayer meetings were not like ones most of us would know – there would be a few designated men only who would be asked to pray.

Everyone at school learned large chunks of the Bible by heart. The influences of the many past revivals had an enormous effect on the lives of the islanders. Their respect for God meant there was hardly any crime on the island, people often left the keys in their cars, peat would be left at the side of the road with no fear of anyone stealing it – difficult for us to imagine these days!

Church on the island is much the same today as it was in the 1940's. There is no music; singing is led by a precentor who is a man and they often sing the Psalms. They have communion in each church twice a year which lasts from Wednesday night to Sunday, and they normally invite an outside minister to conduct the services.

I have been to one where there was singing then the minister spoke, then singing again and the minister spoke again, etc. They separated those who were card-carrying members of the church who were allowed communion and those who were not. As a charismatic Christian, I hated the service and I asked God to get me out of there. He admonished me rather strongly, reminding me that He had started revivals in many of these types of services!

The Church of Scotland and the Free Church had given out an instruction that everyone should pray for revival. This was not difficult for the people were well practised in prayer; it was the basis of the 1934 and 1939 revivals.

Prayer was woven into the very fabric of the church in Barvas and many spontaneous prayer meetings would start as people met with each other in their homes. It was a community at prayer!

> "They came to know the secret of humility, of seeking the Lord, of depending on Him to work, of importunately laying hold of Him, of passionately pleading with Him."

There were signs of revival early in 1949, with people being saved on the island. One pastor declared that it only needed a spark!

The minister at Barvas, James Murray MacKay, invited Duncan Campbell (his second choice) to come over and minister, but he declined due to his busy schedule. Now there were two elderly sisters, one blind, who were amazing intercessors, who the minister respected greatly, and they told him that Campbell would come, so they and the church prayed and on December 7th 1949 Campbell arrived in Barvas, Lewis, a desolate spot, surrounded by peat moors and bogs.

There is a myth across the internet, that came from Campbell's recorded messages, that the Smith sisters prayed in the revival and were solely responsible for Campbell's arrival. This story is untrue, the whole Island was praying in the revival and the whole Barvas church prayed for Campbell to come.

Holy Spirit was not only encouraging people to pray, He also prepared Duncan Campbell. The missioner wrote sometime later:

> "After spending seventeen years in a barren wilderness, baffled and frustrated in Christian work and witness, I suddenly came to realise that God had

made provision for clean hands and a pure heart. And on my face in my own study at five o'clock in the morning I came to know the recovering power of the blood of Christ... I know that in some small measure – the revival in Skye and later in Lewis, must be related to the experience of that morning. What was it that led me into this full realisation of glorious deliverance in the Holy Ghost? I answer in one word, a baptism from God. Explain it as you will, it was a baptism from God. That experience was in my case preceded by a spiritual hunger, a longing for God to do something."

This was the Baptism of Fire that has prepared many people for revival. Holiness is always a vital part of revival as can be seen from the following account about members of the Barvas church:

"Before the revival began some people prayed in a barn for six weeks until a young man declared that the prayers were wasted unless they were right with God. "Then he lifted his two hands and prayed, 'God, are my hands clean? Is my heart pure?' But he got no further. That young man fell to his knees and then fell in a trance and is now lying on the floor of the barn. And in the words of the minister, at that moment, he and his other office bearers were gripped by the conviction that a God sent revival must always be related to Holiness, must ever be related to Godliness. Are my hands clean? Is my heart pure?"

This was just one example of what went on all over the area.

Beginning

The start of the revival is a very well-known story, mainly

because a sermon of Duncan Campbell's, setting out in detail the first night he was at Barvas, was recorded in 1968 and is all over the web.

This account tells of him going directly to the 7pm meeting, the meeting was good but not exceptional and it ended at 10:45pm when people left. A deacon then prayed for God to act and a blacksmith came in to show them the outside of the church where six hundred people were waiting. One hundred of them came from a dance where suddenly the presence of God fell and they all knew they had to go to the church. The meeting started again and went on until 4:00am with many crying out to God and giving their lives to the Lord. Campbell then walked a mile to the police station passing young people at the side of the road on their knees and found four hundred people crying out to God.

An amazing, wonderful story, but in my opinion it is untrue. It pains me to say this of such a respected man, but for some reason Duncan Campbell added everything from the end of the meeting at 10:45pm. Perhaps he put together several experiences into one evening or perhaps his memory was going (he was seventy when he told the story).

In the book 'Sounds from Heaven', there is Campbell's own report to the Faith Mission, at the end of the first week:

> "I began my mission on Wednesday night in the parish church. People gathered from all over the parish and we had a congregation of over 300. The meeting began at 7:00pm and ended at 10.45pm. I preached twice in the evening. This was repeated on Thursday and Friday. Yesterday, I preached in three different churches to crowded meetings. at the last meeting (on Sunday at Shader), the Lord manifested His power in a gracious way and the

cry of the anxious was heard all over the church. I closed the service but people would not go away, so I gathered the anxious ones beneath the pulpit and, along with the minister, did what we could to lead them to Christ."

There is no mention of anything after 10:45pm and no mention of Holy Spirit at work. I do not believe for a second that Campbell would have left out of the report something as amazing as he described twenty years later. In the same book the Barvas minister wrote that the revival broke out in Shader on the Sunday. There are two other similar testimonies in the book which is why I have come to the conclusion that Campbell merged different reports.

It is so disappointing that this erroneous report, as well as the one about the elderly sisters, has been accepted all around the world. However, it is a good lesson for us – never accept anything on the web as truth!! You always need to get more than one source for a story.

At the close of the service at Shader on December 11th some went back to the church to the prayer meeting, to seek the Lord as their Saviour. After the service those who were seeking the Lord were asked to remain. Usually, three men would pray and then Duncan Campbell spoke for fifteen minutes on the way to salvation. Many came to the Lord at this meeting, but some did not and of those a number would find Him on the walk home.

Even more sought Jesus at a house meeting at the home of Donald Morrison where some had gone after the church service. Evidently, a glorious time was had and many more were experienced there in the days and weeks ahead.

Someone wrote about that first week:

"The Spirit of God was resting amazingly and

graciously on these two townships (Shader and Barvas) at that time and His resting was glorious. You could feel him in the homes of the people, on the common and on the moor and even as you walked along the road through the two townships."

The revival spread but one town in Lewis was not responding to the prayer for revival. Arnol is two miles from Barvas and extra prayer was called for, so Duncan Campbell and others went to have an extended prayer meeting in someone's house:

"It was a hard battle as one after another attempted to breakthrough in prayer. Sometime after midnight, Duncan Campbell called upon John Smith (a leading intercessor on the island) to pray. He had not prayed all night. He rose and prayed for some time and then he said:

'Lord, I do not know how Mr Campbell or any of these other men stand with you, but if I know my own heart, I know that I am thirsty. You have promised to pour water on him that is thirsty. If You don't do it, how can I ever believe You again. Your honour is at stake. You are a covenant-keeping God. Fulfil Your covenant engagement.' It was a prayer of a man who was walking with God. At that moment the house shook."

The intercessors on the island were travailers, they pulled heaven down to earth. Someone wrote, "they have come to learn the secret of pressing through into the courtroom of heaven and of touching the throne." Two unsaved neighbours who were listening were saved that night. The meeting had ended and on leaving the house they saw people carrying chairs to the meeting hall, expectant of a revival meeting. The revival in Arnol had begun.

Campbell came across a woman praying by the side of a road at 5.00am one morning. He joined her in prayer for two hours when he discovered she was burdened for revival for her village. Fourteen young men were trying to decide how much drink to bring into the village for the weekend. In a little while all fourteen were converted.

Opposition

As mentioned earlier, the Free Church did not officially join in the revival, although many of their people did. However, the ministers of the Free Church were not happy about this and set up rival meetings and spoke out strongly against the revival. Some even said that Duncan Campbell had been sent by the devil to disrupt the Church. "The opposition was vicious at times and resulted in confusion and bitterness."

There was a lot of history between the Free Church and the Church of Scotland, so when the revival began in a Church of Scotland church through a Church of Scotland minister, there was bound to issues. Campbell was perceived to be a big problem, in that they thought he was an Armenian whereas they were Calvinists. They were therefore desperate to protect their flock from being contaminated by Armenian theology. However, they did not do any checking, because Campbell was not a trained theologian, and his message of 'sin, judgement and salvation,' should have been perfectly acceptable to the Calvinist ministers. Many Free Church people were thrilled by his message.

It happens in all revivals - people make judgements without discerning what is of the Lord and what is not. Tragic!

Characteristics

> "I felt as if the Spirit of the Lord was in the very air one was breathing."

> "Wherever you went you could not get away from the presence of the Lord."

The revival was all about the presence of God. Whether they were in a meeting, walking along a road, in a boat, in a cinema, working in a field – the presence of God was everywhere! An unsaved man said:

> "I don't need to go to the meetings to know that there is something supernatural going on in the village. I feel it in my own home."

This characteristic cannot be overemphasised; people would stop walking or working because they felt the presence all around them!
Then there was the power of God:

> "The atmosphere changed and we were very conscious of the presence of God. Something happened – it was as if the power of God swept through the house. A number came under deep conviction of sin... Wave after wave of Holy Ghost power swept over the meeting and strong men were broken down and crying for mercy."

There were manifestations but they were peripheral. Some fainted or went into trances. The manifestations were more prevalent in the 1939 revival.

The revival was Bible centred, Campbell used to say, "Preach the Word, sing the Word, live the Word."

Duncan Campbell was a powerful, fiery preacher who preached the whole gospel. Someone said that on two visits to hear him he felt that Campbell was addressing him and him alone and that he felt that it was his sin that Campbell was speaking about:

> "Every night the preacher thundered forth the judgements of God. He stormed up and down the pulpit expounding Scripture and preaching damnation to the lost and salvation to those who repented and savingly believed. I knew one thing – this man was sincere."

As mentioned earlier, prayer was as usual absolutely key. People were brought to their knees to birth the 1939 revival and again in 1949. There were those who refused to accept things as they were. Prayer meetings for revival were held in many homes. People believed that the Glory of God would come down and they prayed until He did; people were praying constantly. "It was a community at prayer."

Someone wrote about the time after the new minister arrived in Barvas in April:

> "We prayed mightily. The atmosphere was full of joy and expectancy, but we were praying all the time, praying, praying, praying!"

There was great expectancy, before the revival and during it. The people were united together, expecting the coming of the Lord in their midst:

> "The presence of God was so powerful that you were constantly living in the expectation that something was about to happen."

The 1904 Welsh revival was all about love, but this one was about conviction, like the revivals of the 18th and 19th centuries:

> "It was all about people weeping as they were convicted of sin, they knew that outside of Christ they were damned. They realised their desperate

need for God's mercy and salvation. Some might weep for days before they got through to God and knew the joy of His forgiveness."

They knew that they had to stand before Almighty God and give account. Eternity, heaven and hell were all real:

"The teenagers were not hearing what the preacher was saying for they were sobbing. They were gripped with the impression of the presence of God and the fact of their sins. The Word which they had learned at school suddenly became alive and they knew that they stood guilty at the bar of God."

Singing was another important aspect of the revival. As mentioned, they sang the Word of God and the singing was full of Holy Spirit. One person remarked, "The singing was like fire going through my whole being." and "The singing was simply glorious, it was almost supernatural, full of joy and spiritual power."

Love and unity was another result of the revival. A contemporary said, "We loved everybody! They were all enveloped in the wonderful love of God! We just loved them all." There was also unity between the generations.

The hunger was so great that that people were in meetings every day, early into the morning. After a church service people would adjourn to someone's home The house would be full, with even the staircase used as a seat. Sometimes there would be a third meeting and even though they would only get a small amount of sleep, they did not get tired.

Interestingly there was no sign of healings or tongues as far as I can see.

It was a glorious revival, but the last one we have experienced in the UK. Let what we have learned here help us to bring about an even more powerful one!

From, 'Sounds from Heaven', by Colin and Mary Peckham, published by Christian Focus.

Conclusion

Well, wasn't it exciting to read the incredible stories of past revivals/awakenings? I never tire of reading about the Baptism of Fire, Travailing Prayer and testimonies.

The manifest power of God is amazing! I really hope you have been stirred up and your faith has grown. However, the purpose of this book is not just to give you a Holy Spirit impartation. I pray you will receive a hunger and desire to take an active role to bring about the awakening that is available to us, and to be deeply involved in it when it comes.

There is no more time. We all know that the state of whichever nation you are from is probably the worst it has been in history. We have to act now! There has been a cloud of apathy over the Church for years – this has to be broken so that our societies can be changed.

One of the most important lessons to learn from these accounts is to know the times and season we are in. I believe we have missed several opportunities over the last hundred years; we must not lose another.

I pray that you will go away from this book, fired up and ready to step into your destiny.

MICHAEL MARCEL'S OTHER BOOKS

It Is Time
"In this book Michael raises questions and offers some solutions for the future reformation of the church; including the need for people to turn their faces and gifts towards our society so that it can be changed. You will find this book a worthwhile challenge."

Dr Sharon Stone
Founder and Apostle of Christian International Europe

God's Heart for a Dying Land
'God's Heart for a Dying Land', is a passionate cry from the heart of one who yearns to see the Church take its rightful position in today's society. It is rich in history and would be an invaluable resource for anyone who has a burden for the nation and who wants to translate that into prayer that brings about lasting change.

Agu Irukwu
Senior Pastor, Jesus House for all Nations (RCCG)

Both are available through www.ukwells.org

MICHAEL MARCEL'S OTHER BOOKS

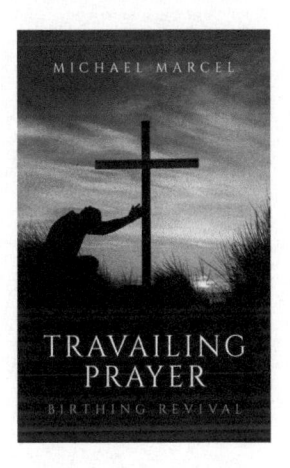

Prepare for Revival

"Revival remains the cry of my heart, a cry which was ignited in a Pastor's House where every Friday night I attended a prayer meeting for Revival, just after I was saved in 1973. It is stirred again as I read. This book will prompt you to prepare and pray for Revival."

Paul Manwaring
Bethel Church Redding, CA.

Travailing Prayer

"There really is an anointing on this book and my spirit gets so stirred as I read. I find myself "eating" the content more than reading it. I deeply connect with this. You have built a beautiful case for the power and fruit of travailing prayer. It's very comprehensive in it's descriptions and content.

Karen

Both are available through www.ukwells.org

BV - #0048 - 070324 - C0 - 216/138/12 - PB - 9781910848562 - Gloss Lamination